WORK
HAPPINESS
Method

By Stella Grizont and available from Headline

The Work Happiness Method

The
WORK
HAPPINESS
Method

STELLA GRIZONT

First published in the USA in 2024 by Hachette Go
an imprint of Hachette Books

First published in Great Britain in 2024 by Headline Home
an imprint of Headline Publishing Group

1

Cataloguing in Publication Data is available from the British Library

Trade paperback ISBN 978 1 0354 1477 2
eISBN 978 1 0354 1478 9

Offset in 10.73/16.95pt Sabon LT Std by Jouve (UK), Milton Keynes

Printed and bound in Great Britain by Clays Ltd, Elcograf S.p.A.

Headline's policy is to use papers that are natural, renewable and recyclable products and made from wood grown in well-managed forests and other controlled sources. The logging and manufacturing processes are expected to conform to the environmental regulations of the country of origin.

HEADLINE PUBLISHING GROUP
An Hachette UK Company
Carmelite House
50 Victoria Embankment
London EC4Y 0DZ

www.headline.co.uk
www.hachette.co.uk

To Ilya, Linor, and Lev, thank you for teaching me what life is all about.

To my parents and the generations of shoulders I stand on, thank you for your strength. I love you.

CONTENTS

ix   PROLOGUE **How This All Started and Why You Need It**

xiii INTRODUCTION **The Eight Inner Skills**

1   CHAPTER 1 **Resilience**
How to Manage Your Mind and Mood

29   CHAPTER 2 **Clarity**
How to Know What You Really, Really Want and
Define Your Unique Vision of Success

41   CHAPTER 3 **Purpose**
How to Make Conscious Decisions with Confidence
and Live Your Values Every Day

62   CHAPTER 4 **Boundaries**
How to Self-Care and Avoid Burnout

92   CHAPTER 5 **Play**
How to Deal with Uncertainty

111 CHAPTER 6 **Discovery**
How to Explore New Roles and Responsibilities

140 CHAPTER 7 **Approach**
How to Transform Confrontations into Conversations

162   CHAPTER 8 **Refocus**
      How to Return to What Matters (Without Pushing So Hard)

177   CONCLUSION **It's Been for You, for All of Us**

181   EPILOGUE **I Believe In You**

182   APPENDIX
189   RECOMMENDED READING
193   NOTES
201   ACKNOWLEDGMENTS

How This All Started and Why You Need It

It was on the floor of my three-hundred-square-foot Hell's Kitchen apartment, in a fetal position, with an empty Nutella jar next to me that I asked myself, "How did I land here again?!" I had spent the previous ten years of my career on a roller coaster, plunging from Corporate America to working for a start-up to running my own business. And despite achieving whatever I put my mind to, I found myself once again burned out, unmotivated, and feeling guilty for polishing off yet another container of chocolate ecstasy—with a tablespoon.

Most likely, you already have a hunch of what I wish I knew back then: that no matter where you work, your issues can follow you. And though maybe you've fantasized about other jobs or even other careers, you have a sneaking suspicion that escaping this one might not be the answer to the fulfillment you seek. What if you leave and get a new job but end up feeling the EXACT SAME WAY?! Yeah, been there and done that. Let me tell you how that went, real quick....

Prior to launching my coaching and training company, I spent nearly ten years in brand strategy. I was paid to listen to people, unearth their deepest desires, and then use those insights to help brands sell better. I thought I was in my dream job, working at one of the world's most prestigious ad agencies, Y&R. I gave it my all and often found myself toiling past midnight, alone in a dark, empty building on Madison Avenue—surviving off a vending machine. I received plenty of recognition and I loved my colleagues, but something was still missing. I didn't feel like I was using my full potential or doing meaningful work. I wanted to do something that I was passionate about. Little by little, it became harder and harder to wake up in the morning. I started catching frequent colds (which was unusual for me). I became depressed and panicked about my career. I started interviewing at other agencies, but it just seemed like more of the same. I didn't know where to go or what I wanted. I just knew I wanted to care about what I did and feel like I was making a difference.

Have you ever been there? Having the "is this all there is?" conversation with God, the universe, or whoever else you speak to when you can't sleep and dread the morning ahead.

Most alarming about this time was that I didn't recognize who I was anymore. I always had given 150 percent to my work, and now I found myself giving 85 percent. My confidence and general enthusiasm were gone. I would come home, reach for the tablespoon, grab for the gorgeous hazelnut chocolate heaven in a jar, and try to numb it all away.

I have a feeling that if you're reading this, you're also an overachiever, but you're not feeling up to overachieving like you used to, am I right?

Eventually, I decided that Corporate America just wasn't for me. I went to work for a start-up that was dedicated to helping women launch their businesses. This was it—or so I thought. I felt like I had found my tribe. I was inspired by the businesswomen I was supporting. I had the opportunity to develop workshops that we offered to over a hundred thousand entrepreneurs. I helped grow our market presence from twenty-four to fifty-four cities across the United States and Canada. And I got to manage and train eighty-eight market leaders. What was most meaningful was the opportunity to personally coach hundreds of women in pursuing their dreams. This couldn't have been a better match for me. But then things started to change. The 2008 recession happened. Our leadership wasn't aligned. I didn't agree with our growth strategy. And, little by little, I began to resent the community that I was once eager to serve. Once again, I found myself nursing a Nutella jar, confused about my future and exhausted by my present.

I decided that if I couldn't find happiness working for other companies and other people, I would work for myself. After helping thousands of other women launch their businesses, I was going to finally launch my own. Inspired by my own state of feeling stuck and miserable at work, I wanted to create an offering that would reignite people, help them break free and be their most alive self at work and in life. To help me understand how to do that, I decided to first go back to school and study the science of happiness, or more formally, Applied Positive Psychology, at the University of Pennsylvania. I was one of the first one hundred people to get a master's degree in happiness. Now I had all the knowledge and tools not only to make myself happy but also to help others. So how was it that just a year after I graduated I was on the floor in my three-hundred-square-foot apartment in the fetal position in a Nutella coma, drowning in imposter syndrome?

I had spent nearly a decade supporting women in launching their dreams, and here I was, sabotaging my own. Although I had a positive start with my business—with clients like Google, Johnson & Johnson, and Aramark—I found myself turning down opportunities because I wasn't motivated to do what I had to do. With a freakin' degree in happiness, here I was, paralyzed by fear, anxiety, and depression. What happened?

Finally, I began to understand one of the most powerful insights that has since freed me and the thousands of people I support each year. I realized that it wasn't Corporate America, the start-up world, the clients, or the leaders I was working with that made me miserable…it was me.

It's been me all along.

So, where does that leave you? Are you, also, at the root of your challenges? I'm not saying that your micromanaging boss isn't the problem or that you don't deserve more recognition or pay or that your company culture doesn't have issues or that you shouldn't strive to make a bigger impact. But what I am saying is that if you really want things to change, you've got to start with you. **Your feeling dissatisfied, bored, miserable, or just unenthusiastic is not all your fault, but it is your responsibility to do something about it.** My goal is to help you become aware of just how damn *powerful* you are and how you have more control than you imagine.

That said, some people have more control than others. Our systems need a lot of work to make things fair and good. This is a small paragraph acknowledging big issues such as discrimination, nonliving wages, lack of good and affordable childcare for all, lack of environmental sustainability, and beyond. Organizations have to do their part because we don't all have time or the means to fight the big fight. Kids need to get to school, lunches need to be made, bills need to be paid— we can't all work on fixing the system or transforming work cultures, but we can all work on ourselves to make a difference. Plus, we can vote. But for now, you and I are going to tackle what's within your reach to help you work happier and live better.

Most of us didn't grow up learning the skills—the inner skills—we need to actually be happy at work and in life. And most aren't learning them on the job now. That's what I'm here to help you with. I'm writing to help you take control where you can.

The Eight Inner Skills

The future of work (and humanity) depends on inner skills. The next frontier is to go within. According to Gallup, 77 percent of employees around the world are feeling unengaged and checking out.[1] This has been the trend since Gallup began measuring engagement in 2009. Feeling blah, meh, bored, or miserable at work not only costs individuals their well-being and happiness but also costs the global economy $8.8 trillion. This equates to 9 percent of global GDP. Imagine what we could achieve if we felt more alive at work.

Today, people want more than just a paycheck from the place where they spend most of their waking hours…they want transformation. They want purpose. They want their effort to matter. They want to love their jobs. Does that resonate with you? Improving our inner skills is the way. *Inner skills* refers to one's ability to relate to oneself. Inner skills aren't a new concept. They just haven't been recognized by institutions and actively developed. It used to be all that mattered were hard skills, which are technical capabilities related to one's tasks. But pure focus on hard skills can lead to toxic work environments and what I call asshole tolerance—when organizations look the other way from inappropriate behavior to realize short-term performance results. Enter soft skills, the ability to relate to others, the capabilities around communication, trust building, leadership, and cooperation. Today, organizations spend $24 billion in helping people develop soft skills.[2] In fact, according to Stanford Research Institute (SRI) International, 75 percent of long-term employment success is driven by mastery of soft skills, while only 25 percent of that success is determined by hard skills. But, despite the spending, employees are still checking out. Something still must change. To break the trend of disengagement, we need a new capability. We have to learn how to relate to ourselves and manage from within. Learning inner skills will release untapped potential in organizations. It will help you feel more fulfilled in your career and in your life.

Inner skills will be regarded as essential workplace skills, especially in the wake of automation and artificial intelligence. According to a McKinsey Global Institute report, demand for inner skills is predicted to grow across all industries by 26 percent in the United States.[3]

Aristotle said, "To know thyself is the beginning of wisdom." Imagine if everyone was self-aware, managed their moods, maintained healthy boundaries, leveraged their strengths, communicated their needs effectively, and was clear on what they really wanted. O.M.G. The world would be a better place! Inner skills, my friend, that's the key to fulfillment—no matter where you work or who you work with.

Until we fortify our inner skills, our issues will follow us wherever we go. I had a client who struggled with saying no to her boss. She was so burned out that she went on sleeping medication just to get some rest. She quit her job and her health rebounded temporarily. Then she found herself back on the same medication within a year at another company. Finally, she learned how to push back and create healthy boundaries—she no longer takes sleeping medication. She loves her job. You can do this, too.

In this book, I'll be teaching you eight critical inner skills to not only cope with your career challenges but also thrive. We'll do this step-by-step together. Here's what we'll cover:

1. **Resilience:** How to manage your mind and mood
2. **Clarity:** How to know what you really, really want and develop your unique vision of success
3. **Purpose:** How to make conscious decisions with confidence and live your values every day
4. **Boundaries:** How to self-care and avoid burnout
5. **Play:** How to deal with uncertainty
6. **Discovery:** How to explore new roles and responsibilities
7. **Approach:** How to transform confrontations into conversations
8. **Refocus:** How to return to what matters (without pushing so hard)

At the end of the day, my mission is to help you live a life worth living and work a job worth your doing. For thousands of years, philosophers, mystics, writers, religious leaders, artists, teachers, teenagers, and poets have wrestled with how to figure that out. Only in the past twenty or so years have scientists actively joined the discussion by way of the field of positive psychology.

Often I'm asked why it is called *positive* psychology—is that as opposed to *negative* psychology? And I say, "No, but kinda." Traditional psychology, which has made great strides in discovering and treating mental illnesses, uses the scientific method to study what's wrong with people and to discover how to get them from a place that's, say, a negative five on a scale of well-being back to zero, or back to "normal." Meanwhile, positive psychology uses the same empirical approach but asks different questions: How do we get people from zero to plus five? How do we help people thrive? Positive psychology is interested in the good life and what it means to flourish. Martin

Seligman, the founder of positive psychology, developed the theory of well-being, a framework to help us understand what drives flourishing.[4] It includes five measurable elements also known as PERMA:

1. *Positive emotion:* Feeling good and being satisfied with your life
2. *Engagement:* Experiencing moments of total absorption, losing track of time and space, being in the flow
3. *Relationships:* Caring about others and knowing that you're cared for, too
4. *Meaning:* Belonging to something bigger than yourself
5. *Achievement:* Developing, mastering, and experiencing a sense of accomplishment

Technically, happiness falls under the first pillar, positive emotion. As you can see, happiness is important, but it's not everything.[5] For example, most parents would agree that taking care of kids isn't always a feel-good experience. In fact, it can be grueling. Yet, it's some of the most fulfilling work there is. The same applies to your career. It won't always feel good, but that doesn't mean it's wrong. It's complex.

In this book, I share the latest research from the fields of positive psychology, leadership studies, neuroscience, and beyond to help you develop your inner skills. I've also included personal stories and stories of some of my clients to bring the tools alive. (I changed the names and identifying details of my clients to honor their privacy.) I suggest you read the chapters in sequential order because the skills build on one another. There are exercises for you to practice using the tools. I encourage you to do them. That's the best way to learn. Always pay attention to your energy. Don't force it. Take what resonates and leave the rest until you're ready. I'll be here for you.

Want to stay organized? To give you more space to write and practice the exercises in this book, I've created downloadable worksheets, templates, and journaling pages to accompany each chapter. They're free and available for you at workhappinessmethod.com/download.

Or scan this QR code with your smartphone.

CHAPTER 1

Resilience

How to Manage Your Mind and Mood

The first inner skill that you'll be developing is resilience, the ability to manage your mind and mood, especially when things don't go your way. Resilience is about integrating, and even growing from, difficult events.

Do any of these experiences resonate?

- You wake up dreading the day ahead.
- You're constantly worried about your next move.
- You can't quite figure out if it's you or your job that's the problem.
- You worry whether you're good enough for your role, your family, or the future you desire.
- You have a hard time being motivated and staying engaged.
- You know you have the potential to do greater things.
- You have trouble being present with your loved ones because work gets in the way.
- You just want to be happy.

Any of these? All of these? Well, the good news is that even if you're stuck in an unideal situation, you actually have more control than you may think to shift it almost immediately. You might not go from 0 to 100, but you can transform enough to gain relief, more brightness, and optimism. That can lead to exploring solutions you didn't see before. Let me tell you about my client Amy.

How Amy Took Control of Her Negative Thinking

Amy is a marketing director for a beauty brand. She was convinced that her boss hated her and that there was no room for her to grow in her job. Depressed about her career, Amy took her anxiety home. She felt guilty because she didn't like who she was around her husband; he was tired of her constant complaining. So, she joined the Work Happiness Method coaching program because she felt lost and questioned whether she was in the right place at work.

After a few weeks, Amy participated in one of our group coaching calls eager to share a breakthrough. She explained how she had worked late for multiple nights to prepare for a presentation that her boss had requested. She arrived early to their 9:00 a.m. meeting, but at 9:05, he wasn't there, and at 9:20, there was still no sign of him. Normally, Amy told us, this would trigger her, sending her down a familiar spiral of feeling disrespected and unworthy and questioning why she was still at this job.

But this time, Amy didn't go there. She noticed herself getting upset and realized she had a number of choices:

1. Get real pissed off.
2. Assume her boss didn't care about her.
3. Enjoy the extra hour in her day and reach out to her boss to understand what had happened.

Before, Amy didn't even realize there were choices! Her reaction would just automatically have been a combo of options 1 and 2. But this time she embraced option 3. Amy was shocked at the difference it made in her day and in her mood. She noticed how much more productive she was and she felt proud that she had avoided a trap.

"Typically, Stella," she said to me, "I would just take it *so* personally and feel depressed for a few days. My husband would be stuck hearing about it over dinner. I can't believe how simple it was to change my thinking."

Wouldn't that be nice? To not let those negative thoughts run you to the ground.

It's Hard to Resist Negative Thoughts Because We All Have a Negativity Bias

Anything that is bad, wrong, or threatening is like Velcro to your attention. That's natural. Let's say you completed a project and nine people told you "great work" and one person didn't like your results. What would you focus on? Probably that one person.

We all have a negativity bias that we inherited from our cavepeople ancestors. It evolved as a survival instinct. Imagine being in the wilderness alone and hearing a rustling in the bushes. You have two options: assume it's just a pretty little bird and stay put, or worry that it's a large carnivorous beast and run away. The folks who assumed the worst ended up surviving. Those are our ancestors, the ones on constant alert to threats. You and almost everyone else have inherited this disposition. Researchers have found that our brain can compute losses faster than it can calculate gains.[1] It's also much easier for us to change our minds from seeing something as a good experience to seeing it as a bad one. Meanwhile, the reverse—shifting our perspective from bad to good—is harder to do.

Now thankfully, if you're reading this book, you're not just looking to survive but are looking to thrive. To thrive, you must be aware of your thoughts and your mind's biases. It takes work, but you can change your mind, shift your perspective, and hack your thinking to be more resilient. When we notice our thoughts, a space in between each thought emerges. Instead of just reacting and going on automatic (which usually doesn't end well), you can occupy that in-between space and intentionally see your options and make a conscious choice rather than a fearful one. It's in that sliver of greater awareness where your new reality can grow.

Now what does this have to do with your experiencing more happiness and fulfillment at work? Did you know that your brain can process forty bits of information per second? But, meanwhile, your body is receiving eleven million bits of information per second.[2] "What your brain attends to becomes your reality," Shawn Achor, a positive psychology researcher and author, said, "and the best way to change your reality is to first realize that there are multiple realities from which you can choose."[3] Translation: If you're not feeling engaged, passionate, balanced, peaceful, joyful, or energized at work or in life, you may not need to quit, start a new career, turn your world upside down, or book a one-week silent retreat. You may not need to go anywhere to discover your aliveness again. All you may need to do is adjust how you perceive your reality.

Proust said, "The real voyage of discovery consists not in seeking new landscapes but in having new eyes."[4] And that starts with which thoughts you think and which emotions you feel. You actually have more choices than you realize. What if sweet possibilities exist right now in your circumstances that you just can't see in the moment? It could be that your brain is choosing not to pay attention to them because your vision is influenced by how you feel. Literally.

The Mood Lens

If you want to see more possibilities for your career, start by changing your mood. It changes what you perceive.

Researchers have found that our emotions change how we look at the world.[5] In one study, one group of students was induced into a positive mood and the other into a negative mood. How did they induce their moods? Simple, they showed the positive group stimuli such as pictures of puppies and babies while the negative group was shown very dark and depressing imagery. It's easy to manipulate your emotions—which is why I want you to consciously tend to them.

Back to the study. After their moods were primed, the study participants put on eye-tracking goggles and looked at a screen where images were flashed. Researchers could then analyze whether a participant's mood influenced where their eyes focused. It turned out that participants in a negative mood tended to focus on one point inside the image. Those in a positive mood first glanced at the periphery of the screen and then their eyes would flit across the entire image. When you're in a positive mood, you literally can see the big picture. You see more possibilities. When you're in a bad mood, you have tunnel vision. It's no wonder why when you're feeling stuck, you stay stuck. It's just that you're not seeing the solution, even if it's right there in front of you.

The Positive of Negative Emotions

Negative emotions do have an upside, though. In fact, it's unhealthy to be happy all the time.

Negative emotions aren't bad; they're data points. Negative emotions are critical for survival. If we didn't feel fear and the urge to run upon seeing a pack of wolves rounding the corner, or if we didn't feel disgust when tasting a spoiled piece of fish, or if we didn't want to fight when experiencing injustice, we'd find ourselves in some very tricky situations. Negative emotions help alert us to something that is wrong and urge us to action.

When negative emotions come up, many folks choose to distract, numb, or suppress them. The message from society is often "just get over it" or "be cool." But, like trying to push a ball under water, your feelings eventually pop to the surface with intensity if they've been repressed. Studies from the University of Texas and Harvard School of Public Health have shown that chronically repressing your emotions can lead to health problems and chronic disease.[6]

We'll discuss the impact of repressed emotions and stress on your physical well-being in more depth in Chapter 4 when we review burnout and boundaries. The ultimate resilience challenge is: How do you deal with negative emotions in a healthy way? The best method for dealing with a negative emotion is to go through it and to experience it with self-compassion.

Self-Compassion

Start with your heart.

If you feel guilty, ashamed, mad, or bad when you suffer a setback, begin with self-compassion. Kristin Neff, a lead researcher in this area, describes self-compassion as having three components:[7]

Acknowledging struggle. Simply label your feelings without trying to change them. It's a mindful approach where we observe our experience without overidentifying with it. This supports us in several ways. First, when we feel negative emotion, it usually occurs in the fear center of the brain, the amygdala. By labeling the feeling, we reduce activity in the amygdala and redirect it to our prefrontal cortex, our planning and action center. This helps relieve our sense of distress because we move from our fight-or-flight brain center to our planning one.[8] We empower ourselves to better deal with the situation at hand. When we specify the emotion, we give ourselves a pathway to alleviate the situation.

It's easy to generalize, for example, by saying, "I'm so stressed at work." Try to get more specific, like this: "I'm uncomfortable asking for help, but I can't do this all on my own." The more nuanced you can get, the more information you will receive about how to alleviate the situation. Interestingly, most people have limited vocabulary when it comes to feelings, but the more we practice, the more fluent we become. See the emotion list in the workhappinessmethod.com/download (link and QR code shown earlier) to help you identify and label what you are feeling. It could sound like this: "I'm noticing anxiety come up as I think about how much more I have left to write."

Being gentle toward the self. Treat yourself as you would treat a dear friend. Imagine a friend is having a hard time at work. We don't beat them up and tell them how much they suck. We try to offer comfort with warmth. This doesn't mean we convince them of their innocence if they've made a mistake, but rather we remind them of their strengths and how they have so much to offer despite a setback. We listen to them and let them share whatever comes up. We ask them how we can help. This is how we can also be toward ourselves when something goes wrong: "Oh, Stella, it looks like you're feeling *anxious*. You didn't realize how much work it would take to write this book. You never wrote a book before! What do you need right now? What would feel comforting to you?" Tend to yourself the way you would a dear friend.

Embracing our humanity. All humans suffer, fail, and are imperfect. This part of self-compassion is about accepting that we don't always get our way or get it right. Self-compassion is not self-pity. When we experience pity, we tend to isolate and feel like we're the only one with such struggles. We feel like a victim. When we have self-compassion, we relate to the vulnerability and frailty of all beings: "Oh, Stella. I'm pretty sure most writers hit a wall when writing. Especially first-time writers."

This type of work takes practice. But just attempting it is a success. It means we're aware enough to know that we can choose how to respond to the moment. It means we're not so identified with the negative emotion that it's completely dominating our consciousness. It signals that we've created spaciousness between our thoughts, which is essential for knowing how to manage them. Progress!

Self-Compassion

1. **Acknowledge struggle:** Label your feelings without trying to change them.
2. **Be gentle toward the self:** Treat yourself as you treat a dear friend.
3. **Embrace your humanity:** Remember we all suffer, fail, and are imperfect.

Now watch out. There are three common traps that trigger our negativity bias and sabotage our happiness and success. I call this trifecta of self-sabotage the Three Cs: complaining, criticism, and comparison. We'll cover two of them now and one in the next chapter.

Knowing how to break free from these three traps bolsters your ability to manage your mind and stay resilient. Here, accompanying a description of the first two traps, I offer you two tools to neutralize them: the Complaint Vacation and the gratitude journal.

Complaining

"Complaining is like bad breath, you notice it when it comes out of someone else's mouth, but not your own," says author and motivational speaker Will Bowen.[9]

So, what do I mean by complaining? Complaining is a state of grievance; it's not just noticing what's wrong but embodying the energy of what's wrong. For example, I could say, "Uggghhhh, it's SOOO hooooot outside!" Or I could say, in a matter-of-fact way, "It's hot outside."

TRAP 1 OF THE NEGATIVITY BIAS

When we're complaining, we're compounding our suffering. The suffering results from identifying with the strong negative emotion that we feel. Complaining is a sign that we have temporarily lost contact with our greater awareness. In fact, it usually signals that we're resisting it.

Complaining is a trap that drags us into a negativity vortex, loosening our grip on the real truth of who we are, forcing us to feel like a victim. Because it triggers and amplifies our negativity bias, everything good, joyful, and meaningful loses its color and we feel like we're out of choices. When we complain, we're not just focusing on what's wrong but have become captive to our feelings about it, and we've forgotten how powerful we are.

Not only does complaining bring us down, but we also take others with us! Did you know that your emotions are contagious, just like the flu? Researchers have found that moods spread, and if you're a leader, your mood spreads even faster.[10]

Again, I'm not saying that you should avoid feeling negative emotions. Not at all. And there's no shame in feeling depressed, angry, upset, resentful, or miserable. The problem is not with experiencing negative emotion but with how we respond to it. Complaining is the gluttony of our ego, it's the overindulgence of negative emotions, it's the loss of consciousness amid pain.

So, how do we break free from the trap of complaining or avoid it altogether? Take a Complaint Vacation.

The Complaint Vacation

I'm so generous with my clients. I give each one an all-expenses-paid vacation...from complaining, that is! And you get one, too! This seven-day luxurious stay comes with peace, increased awareness of your thoughts, and all-you-can-sigh relief, knowing that your job and life are so much better than you imagined. Cue the applause!

Being on a Complaint Vacation means that any time you notice yourself about to launch into an episode of complaining, you remind yourself of your glorious stay and say, "I'm taking a break from complaining this week." When you acknowledge your vacation, you are operating from your greater awareness because you're noticing your thoughts. This gives you just enough space to reduce the emotional inflammation caused by whatever event just triggered you.

Practicing the Complaint Vacation helps you recognize the power you have over your mind. You'll start to frequent the space in between your thoughts more regularly. Even if you don't always choose the complaint-free vacation but are aware that you're *not* choosing it, that's progress.

Take a Complaint Vacation

TOOL

Any time you notice yourself about to launch into an episode of complaining, remind yourself: "I'm taking a break from complaining this week."

The Gratitude Journal

Well, if complaining is about focusing on what's wrong and embodying the upset, gratitude is about noticing what's right and feeling appreciation. Numerous studies show that gratitude is one of the strongest predictors of positive mental health. It can dissipate the strong hold of our negativity bias. People who are grateful are more satisfied with their relationships with friends and family. They're happier, less depressed, and less stressed. They feel more in control of their lives, have higher self-esteem, and cope better with setbacks. Grateful people are better at learning from tough experiences. They're less likely to avoid problems, deny that anything's wrong, or blame themselves. That's also probably why grateful people sleep better!

Dr. Robert Emmons, with the University of California, Davis, has been at the forefront of research on gratitude.[11] He found that people who kept a gratitude journal on a weekly basis exercised more regularly, reported fewer physical symptoms, felt better about their lives, and were more optimistic about the upcoming week compared to those who recorded hassles or neutral life events. In a study conducted by Drs. Martin Seligman, Tracy Steen, Nansook Park, and Christopher Peterson, a group of people were asked to practice a gratitude exercise every day for one week.[12] Even though the exercise lasted just one week, at the one-month follow-up, participants were happier and less depressed than they had been at baseline, and they stayed that way at the three- and six-month follow-ups. We know gratitude is important…but are you actively practicing it?

TOOL

Gratitude Journal

Notice what's good and right, especially when things feel wrong. See those people, events, or things as gifts. Write it down. For one week, try writing down five points of gratitude per day. Use the journaling sheets from workhappinessmethod.com/download to track your gratitude.

Any Questions?

I have some answers! See the following.

When should I do my gratitude exercises?

In his book *Tiny Habits*, world-renowned behavior scientist at Stanford University B. J. Fogg recommends that if you want to create a new habit, anchor it to something that you do every day.[13] For example, do your gratitude after brushing your teeth, pouring your coffee, or climbing into bed.

Pick an anchor now so you don't have to decide later:

▶ I will practice my gratitude every day after or before I _____

_____.

What if I can't find anything to be grateful for?

You can train your brain to see the glass as half full. Our mind might be so used to focusing on what's wrong that it misses seeing what's right. Did you know that our brain can create new neural pathways and delete old ones, which means that it is always changing? This quality is called neuroplasticity. Our brain can grow and can also languish. By choosing to focus on what's going well, we create a new neural pathway. It might start off like a dirt path, but the more we travel on it, the smoother it gets until eventually it's a highway! Soon, identifying what's good feels natural and easy.

I once had a client who said his whole worldview changed after taking his Complaint Vacation and coupling it with gratitude. As a senior researcher, George complained that his office culture was toxic. He felt like he was being swallowed up by everyone's negativity. Once he started doing the gratitude practice, he noticed wonderful things about his work that he hadn't paid attention to before. For example, at a previous job he had trouble finding parking and had to leave his house twenty minutes earlier just to find a spot. Now, he gets more sleep and pulls right up to his office. He also appreciates how he gets to collaborate with top talent in his industry. He realizes how lucky he is to have his own lab to work in, which has always been a dream. He went from deep angst to feeling fortunate in less than a week. Did this change everything he hated about his work culture? No, but it dramatically shifted how he felt each day. That's a start.

What about you? What might you be taking for granted at the office or in your life? Examples could be free coffee, a functioning computer, flexibility to work from home, a boss who cares, heat, air-conditioning, clean water, or a paycheck that comes on time. This exercise alone might not solve all your problems, but it can help you see more and differently enough to figure them out.

▶ Let's start now. Capture five things you are grateful for today and describe why:

1. _____

_____

_____

2. _____

_____

_____

3. _____

_____

_____

4. _____

_____

_____

5. _____

_____

_____

Notice how your body feels during your gratitude practice. Observe yourself without judgment. If you had difficulty, that's fine.

Okay, I can come up with a list, but what if I don't really feel grateful?

Just fake it. I do it all the time! Do you think I feel like doing my gratitude practice on days when I'm grumpy and tired? I drag myself to the practice. Just like getting yourself to the gym is the hardest part, so is starting to write or think about gratitude, especially if you're not in the mood. Initially, you'll list things that you intellectually know you should be grateful for: health, friends, family, a home. If your mind is saying: "Blah, blah, blah, so what? I'm still cranky and this isn't helping!" consider an exercise I call "Free Thanking." In high school we'd have freewriting sessions where you weren't allowed to stop writing until the teacher called time. Your pen had to remain in motion, writing whatever came to mind. When I'm really in a funk, I employ the same method for my gratitude: I keep writing my gratitude for five or ten minutes. By the time I stop, my eyes are watery and my heart is singing.

You can also get some help. Because our emotions are contagious, ask your team to share one good thing at the top of a meeting. Let their gratitude and positivity rub off on you!

Criticism

One of my clients, Mariel, is a scientist who graduated from an Ivy League school and holds a prestigious position at an energy company. All of her colleagues have PhDs, but Mariel does not. She constantly put herself down because of it. Haunted by her inner critic, this accomplished woman perpetually felt like she wasn't good enough. She was so afraid to fail that she didn't put herself out there and then punished herself

TRAP 2 OF THE NEGATIVITY BIAS

for not taking risks. Her inner critic held her back from taking on exciting leadership opportunities and doing activities she loved, such as creative writing. Even her fiancé was having a hard time dealing with her incessant insecurity.

Imposter syndrome is the disease of overachievers.

Have you ever felt like you didn't deserve to be where you are? Have you worried that you're a fraud and that at any minute they're going to figure you out? This is called imposter syndrome and it usually affects high performers. Essentially, it means you have a hard time ascribing your success to your own effort: you may think that you got lucky, someone did you a favor, or they haven't figured you out yet. Whether or not you have imposter syndrome like Mariel or like I had (remember me, the happiness expert who was so depressed that she numbed herself with Nutella?), I bet you have an active inner critic.

Self-criticism is the second mental trap I am warning you about. Because just as Mariel held herself back, you may be doing the same. Although our inner critic might disguise itself as tough love, pointing out our flaws, just trying to help us be better, it can end up destroying our confidence, success, and happiness. We each have an inner critic, but for some of us that voice becomes too loud and unmanageable, so much so that it leads to a condition called learned helplessness.

Coined by Martin Seligman, former president of the American Psychological Association and one of the founders of Applied Positive Psychology, *learned helplessness* describes a condition brought on by persistent setbacks, trauma, or failure.[14] It causes people to give up trying to change because they feel powerless.

When animal trainers taught elephants to stay put in the circus, they'd induce learned helplessness. A trainer would tie a rope around a baby elephant's neck and secure that to

(continues)

(continued)

a post. No matter how much the baby elephant tugged or resisted, it couldn't break free. Eventually, the trainer didn't have to secure the rope to a post. With just the rope around its neck, the elephant no longer believed that it could escape and it stopped trying. Even once it was fully grown, the elephant never realized that it had the strength and power to break free.

Check in with yourself. Is there a corner in your career or personal life where you feel like "no matter what I do, it's always going to be this way"?

- No matter how many times I try to get on the Anderson account, they're going to say no.
- No matter how many times I tell Ed we need more staff, he won't make room in the budget.
- No matter how many diets I try, I'll never keep off the weight.
- No matter how hard I work, I won't be able to get ahead.

Sometimes learned helplessness is difficult to spot because we just can't imagine the situation being any other way. Having an unchecked inner critic often coincides with a pessimistic explanatory style. *Explanatory style* is a fancy way of saying "how we talk to ourselves." Seligman noticed that when something goes wrong, folks experiencing learned helplessness tend to explain the situation with the following Three Ps:

1. **It's personal:** What happened is all my fault because I'm not good enough.
2. **It's permanent:** This crappy situation isn't going to change. It will always be this way.
3. **It's pervasive:** Not only did this go wrong, but also now all these other things will go wrong.

Do you ever find yourself thinking along these lines? Imagine who you could be if you broke free from this mental trap. Imagine how much energy you'd free up and what you could do with it.

In the following, I offer you a tool to throw off the imaginary rope tying you down. It's called Learned Optimism.

Learned Optimism

The good news is that just as we can learn to feel helpless and give up, we can also learn to be powerful. Remember that plastic brain of yours—it can create, edit, and delete neural pathways. According to Seligman's research, one way to quiet our inner critic is to change the dialogue we have with ourselves from one of learned helplessness to one of learned optimism.

I liken practicing learned optimism to participating in a legal trial of *You v. Your Inner Critic*. In that trial, you have to play the defense attorney and prove these three things: this situation is *not* personal, permanent, or pervasive.

Let's review an example of how learned helplessness versus learned optimism might sound in your mind. Imagine you didn't turn in a report on time:

Personal Versus Not Personal

Learned Helplessness: "I'm such a loser and it's all my fault."

Learned Optimism: "I didn't have enough time this week because I was working on multiple projects at once. This doesn't mean I don't have what it takes to be successful or that my report wasn't good. I just need to learn how to manage my time better."

Permanent Versus Not Permanent

Learned Helplessness: "I'm always running late."

Learned Optimism: "I ran late on the report and that sucks. But I've handed in plenty of assignments on time before, too."

Pervasive Versus Not Pervasive

Learned Helplessness: "I'm doomed to always be late. I'm never going to get that promotion, my kid won't be able to go to a good school, my wife is going to be pissed. Why did she even marry me? I'm a crap leader. My team is disappointed in me, too."

Learned Optimism: "I know I have other strengths and have had other wins this quarter. I'm also a great leader and my team still has faith in me. This was a blow, but my job and paycheck are secure."

TOOL

Learned Optimism

When you suffer a setback and your inner critic is convinced it will always be this way, reframe the event with Learned Optimism by saying this to yourself:

What happened isn't great, but its impact is . . .

- **Not personal**—this doesn't define me as a human being.
- **Not permanent**—this won't last forever; it can be different next time.
- **Not pervasive**—this won't impact every aspect of my career or life.

Now it's your turn. Is there any area where you feel like you're stuck and no matter what you do, it will never change? Maybe it's about getting recognition, a promotion, or a date? Put on your defense attorney hat and prove to yourself that what happened is *not* personal, *not* permanent, and *not* pervasive.

Event: _____

This is *not* personal because _____ .

This is *not* permanent because _____ .

This is *not* pervasive because _____ .

Questions?

What if I can't think of an example of my inner critic wreaking havoc?

Our inner critic is wildly creative. It might not seem like helplessness but come in a different form. Just keep the Three Ps of learned optimism—it's not personal, permanent, and pervasive—handy for when something comes up and you find yourself feeling stuck. Self-compassion is always a good go-to as well.

What if I still believe that things won't change?

Rewiring your circuitry takes time and practice. You might want to consider working with a coach or therapist. There's nothing wrong with getting support. Eventually, this way of thinking will become more natural. Please give yourself credit for practicing—that's progress.

But isn't this just a way of not taking responsibility for how I messed up?

It's always important to acknowledge what role you played in any situation, even if it was just 1 percent. This isn't about shirking responsibility or accountability; this is about *not* beating yourself up for an error in a nonproductive fashion. It relates to self-compassion in that it keeps you from overidentifying with the setback.

Is there anything I can do preemptively to avoid these traps?

Maintain what I call the Boring Basics. This book guides you in growing your inner skills to control what you can control. To even have the mental power to do that, you have to create circumstances for optimal well-being. Too much stress makes us less resilient. The Boring Basics are the fundamentals that maintain our mental fortitude, self-control, and health. In our brain, our self-control center resides in the prefrontal cortex. Certain activities deplete it and others strengthen it. I know you know these are important, and here's a loving reminder to take care of them if you're not already.

The Boring Basics

TOOL

The Boring Basics are stuff we all know we should be doing but sometimes forget to do. They're obvious, simple, and they work. So it's incredibly annoying that for some reason we don't always tend to these basics. Ready for your gentle nudge? Drumroll, please . . . the Boring Basics include breathing, sleeping, eating, drinking water, exercising, meditating, experiencing nature, and loving.

The Boring Basics

Breathing

Your breath is always available to you.[15] Unlike your heartbeat or digestion, this is one automatic function that you can directly and immediately influence (even in the middle of a meeting). Breathing more quickly or less deeply in response to a stressful event can cause even more stress! But you can control your breath to help control your mind. Many ancient traditions knew this and science validates the impact breath can have on mood.

A recent study at Stanford by David Spiegel, Andrew Huberman, and Melis Yilmaz Balban, and others shows that a particular type of breath called cyclic sighing is especially effective in reducing anxiety.[16] To try it, take a deep breath in through your nose until you've comfortably filled your lungs. Then, take a second, deeper sip of air to expand your lungs even more. Very slowly, exhale completely through your mouth until all the air is gone. You'll feel more relaxed with just a few rounds of this breath. Keep it going for five minutes a day and you will experience more positive emotion throughout your day.

Consciously controlling your breathing, especially giving yourself long exhales, activates your parasympathetic nervous system and shifts you out of a stress response by slowing down your heart rate and generating calm throughout your entire body.

Sleep

You can't get more boring, basic, or essential than sleep. Our prefrontal cortex, our command center, can't absorb fuel (glucose) efficiently when we're undersleeping. Studies have found that after seventeen to nineteen hours without sleep, we're operating like a drunk driver who has a blood alcohol level of 0.05 percent.[17] Although we may *know* how to respond appropriately to a setback, if we don't have the mental reserves, we can't marshal the willpower to execute.

There are tons of great resources, tools, and brilliant hacks to support your rest and sleep hygiene.[18] Here are the basics: do your best to avoid electronic screens two hours before bedtime; go to bed at the same time every night, ideally before 11:00 p.m., to support your circadian rhythm; and shoot for at least seven hours of rest. Easier said than done.

Sometimes you don't have a choice. My son didn't sleep through the night until he was two years old. Everything was harder and darker in my life during that time. When I'm underslept, I'm a much grumpier and short-tempered person. I find myself procrastinating and getting distracted easily. Do what you can when you can.

Sometimes you do have a choice but just don't want to go to bed. This is what TikTok is calling "revenge bedtime procrastination." We've all done it. Basically, it's when we opt to stay up late to watch a show, scroll on our phone, or do whatever to get revenge on the busyness of our day. It's opting for me-time at the expense of sleep. I'm guilty of this. After my kids are in bed and the dishes are washed, I have less than an hour of downtime. It doesn't feel like enough. Plus, my husband and I are both night owls, so it's hard. I just keep reminding myself of how much more kind, effective, and joyful I am when I've rested and I get myself to bed. My progress is slow, but it's getting better.

Food

As I mentioned, our brain uses glucose to function. If our brain detects a shortage of glucose in our body, it will reserve resources and cut back on activities that require more energy. Self-control requires a lot of energy. The amount of self-control we have is finite. Making our dreams come true and being the kind of person we want to be take a lot of work planning, decision-making, and saying no.

Maintaining a low glycemic diet and avoiding concentrated sweets so that glucose is gradually released into the bloodstream help our brain maintain a steadier supply of energy. Do your best to avoid foods that spike and crash your blood sugar levels—like foods with added sugar and simple carbohydrates. Wonky blood sugar levels mess with your hormones and your ability to manage your mind and mood. I know this is basic advice, and of course consult your doctor and choose what's right for you. But, generally speaking, opting for meals and snacks of unprocessed foods that consist of lean proteins, fresh vegetables and fruits, and complex carbohydrates is better than spoonfuls of Nutella.

Hydration

We can't survive without water, so it makes sense that being dehydrated can impact our mind and mood. Water affects every cell in our body. Drinking water is important for all bodily functions, especially our brain's. Multiple studies have found a relationship between dehydration and depression and anxiety.[19] Our nervous system requires water to function properly. It helps deliver signals and nutrients to the brain, remove toxins, and reduce inflammation.

Drink your water—not only will it support your emotional well-being but also your skin will look great! In terms of how much, the amount you should drink depends on your size, activity level, and the weather.[20] Every day try to drink between half an ounce and an ounce of water for each pound you weigh. For example, if you weigh 200 pounds, drink 100 ounces of water. If you plan to work out, if it's hot outside, or if you're drinking coffee, increase your intake.

Exercise

Exercise is one of the most effective behavioral techniques to support self-regulation. It immediately improves mood, attention, and energy. Studies have found that a long-term effect of exercise is that it helps grow your prefrontal cortex.[21] Bam! Try to go for thirty minutes of moderate activity a day. Get your heart rate up a nudge, but don't overdo it. In fact, too much strenuous exercise can cause negative stress in the body.

When it comes to movement, anything is better than nothing. Start with the smallest amount you can consistently do and go from there. One of my clients chose to walk to his mailbox every day as a start. What's your small start if you need one?

Meditation

The key to avoiding the three mental traps I describe in this book is to grow your mental awareness and thereby your emotional competence. *Emotional competence* refers to your ability to recognize, interpret, and constructively respond to your own emotions and others'.[22] The best ways to develop emotional competence is through practicing any of the tools I share with you. They all require mindful awareness.

You can also become more mindful by practicing meditation. I know you know this, but here's your gentle reminder to either start a meditation practice or reengage in your practice if you've gotten off track. Any form of meditation that slows you down and focuses your attention helps you build the mental strength to resist the weight of your negativity bias. The key is to consciously choose how you respond to the events in your work and life. Sometimes we can't even control that, depending on how our nervous system is wired (more on that in Chapter 4), but we can control how we respond to our response.

Mindfulness will help you feel your emotions, discern what's true and what's a story you're replaying for yourself, and choose appropriately between them. You may want to experiment with different forms of meditation until you find what feels right for you. Find an app and start with guided meditations. Keep trying until you get into a groove. Just remember the goal is not to "empty your mind"; the goal is to keep returning to your focal point—whether that's your breath, a visual, the sensations in your body. The practice is managing your attention and noticing it without judgment. Sitting in that space of observation is your control center. Occupy that more often and you'll become more resilient.

Nature

Spending time in nature can support your well-being, mood, and relationships. In 1982, Tomohide Akiyama, director of the Japanese Forestry Agency, coined a term to describe the activity of spending time in a forest: *shinrin-yoku*, or "forest bathing."[23] *Shinrin-yoku* involves using your five senses to be present with the trees. Gaze at the patterns of branches, feel the texture of the tree bark, smell the fresh pine scent, listen to the birds. Being present with the forest is now increasingly recommended as a form of preventative care.

Researchers found that exposure to nature—in person or even via video (of course spending time outside had stronger effects)—leads to improvements in attention, positive emotions, and the ability to reflect on a life problem.[24] Another study in Denmark found that children who lived in neighborhoods that included more green space had a reduced risk of many psychiatric disorders later in life, including depression, mood disorders, schizophrenia, eating disorders, and substance use disorder.[25] Those with exposure to the lowest levels of green space during childhood had a 55 percent higher risk of mental illness than those who grew up with abundant green space. Nature also makes us nicer. One experiment found that elementary schoolchildren acted more pro-socially to classmates and strangers after a field trip to a nature school than to an aviation museum.[26] Get some fresh air—so basic, so worthwhile.

Loving Connection

People matter.[27] That's the basic truth. Social bonds change how we perceive the world. Having a friend by your side makes challenges seem less challenging. Researcher Simone Schnall and her colleagues asked a group of people to estimate the steepness of a hill.[28] People in the control group stood alone while people in the experimental group got to stand with a friend by their side. Those with social support estimated the hill to be less steep. Even just imagining a friend by their side had the same effect. This is why people who have a best friend at work are more engaged, satisfied with their job, and likely to stay at their company.[29]

When you feel overwhelmed, plug back into your relationships. Work in the office together. Turn your cameras on when videoconferencing. Call up a friend. Or spend some quiet moments visualizing your loved ones surrounding you, cheering you on.

Togetherness puts our nervous system at ease and helps us metabolize our stress, whereas loneliness produces stress in our body.[30] We need to be in warm, caring relationships to survive or we risk premature death. The problem is that we experience a vicious cycle around loneliness. When we're stressed, we tend to isolate, which creates more stress and further isolation. If you're feeling all alone, hack the momentum of isolation and reach out to someone you care about.

It's not just our strong social ties that matter. In fact, our weak social ties matter just as much. Assessing the social interactions and happiness of over fifty thousand people, a recent study shows that interacting with a more diverse set of relationship types predicts higher well-being.[31] That means that positively interacting with a stranger, the grocery checkout clerk, and the person in accounting also fills our cup and contributes to our well-being. We need to experience both strong and weak ties and, ideally, in even amounts. This not only helps diminish stress in our body but also amplifies our well-being. Consider chitchat before a meeting starts an investment in your social portfolio with dividends of happiness. Just as you seek out healthy foods, intentionally seek out connections to nourish yourself. Togeth-erness gives robustness to our individual resilience.

Tending to the basics are table stakes. If you're not tending to them, everything is so much harder. When you're noticing yourself feeling off, ask yourself: Am I at least getting the basic package? Am I tired, lonely, hungry, or thirsty? Sometimes all you need is a simple fix.

My client Mariel, the scientist, joined the Work Happiness Method coaching sessions because, she said, "I felt inferior and that negativity killed my self-confidence. I felt stuck and like I would never progress or fulfill my potential." Thanks to developing the inner skill around how to manage her mind, Mariel has since flourished. She stopped beating herself up all the time, and that gave her wings. She was nom-inated into a leadership rotation program, she started creative writing again, and she generally feels excited to go to work in the morning. She's no longer obsessing about whether she needs another degree and she's focused on her work. Your reality can also shift.

Resilience Practice

- Take a Complaint Vacation for seven days. If you end up complaining, just remind yourself that you're on vacation.
- Write down five things you are grateful for each day for seven days.
- If your inner critic sounds, speak back to it with self-compassion and learned optimism: "This setback is not personal, pervasive, or permanent."
- Check in on your Boring Basics. Which one, if any, needs the most support? What's the tiniest improvement you can make over the next seven days? Write that down here:

_____

As you practice, notice what you notice. Pay attention to which thoughts or feelings come up. The more you notice, the more aware you become and the more control you have over your responses.

CHAPTER 2

Clarity

How to Know What You Really, Really Want and Define Your Unique Vision of Success

In Chapter 1, we talked about two mental traps, two of the Three Cs that sabotage your happiness and success: complaining and criticism. Now let's discuss *the* mental trap of the twenty-first century, the third C: comparison. If you have a TikTok, Instagram, or LinkedIn account, it's almost impossible not to compare yourself to others. How many times have you gotten lost on social media and then found yourself feeling crappy afterward? I call it an insecurity hangover. Even though you know it gets to you, it's hard to avoid comparing yourself to others. In psychology, the desire to gauge how we stack up relative to others is described as *social comparison*.

In this chapter, we're going to talk about comparison and how clarity of your vision and values can extricate you from this trap. Knowing your vision sets you free to make choices that genuinely support your happiness and fulfillment.

Comparison

On its own, comparison isn't good or bad, it's data gathering. But very rarely is it objective or fair. With the help of your mighty inner critic, comparison becomes an exercise in self-judgment. So, instead of just observing your friend's Instagram-worthy new kitchen, their epic trip to Iceland, or their lobster dinner on Martha's Vineyard, you start telling yourself how you're never going to have enough, do enough, or be enough.

TRAP 3 OF THE NEGATIVITY BIAS

Comparison rarely ends well because it feeds our hungry inner critic. I've spent so much time in the comparison trap—weeks, months, even years feeling a black cloud hover over me. I look back and have compassion for myself and mourn those moments when, instead of celebrating my strengths, I pummeled my confidence. It doesn't have to be this way and I hope I can help you break free from this trap. Here's how!

The thing with comparison is that we look outside of ourselves to gauge where we stand. So, the way to avoid entering this defeating game is to put your blinders on and look inward. When horses wear blinders, they're prevented from looking back and to the side. Where should your gaze rest? I want your eyes planted on your path ahead only. What does your finish line look like? It's a vision of you being your most alive, joyful, energized, peaceful, fulfilled YOU. It's setting your eyes on your unique vision of success.

The inner skill of clarity is knowing your vision. Your vision is a statement that describes you at your best, feeling your best. When you think of being successful, your vision describes it in its purest form. That is what you want to be measuring yourself against and inching toward each day. Instead of comparing yourself to others, compare yourself to your own vision of how you (not your mom, friends, boss, or society) want to be.

Your Vision

The big mistake people make when it comes to their goals is first thinking about what they want to achieve. Your vision is not a list of achievements but an expression of your being fulfilled. When people think about success, they imagine what they want to accomplish: getting that VP title, being paid more money, buying a new home, winning awards, or finally letting go of tedious tasks. Often, even if they achieve those goals, they can find themselves feeling underwhelmed with a sense of "is this all there is?"

The problem—and this isn't anyone's fault—is that we've all been choosing our goals using backward logic by first identifying a desired achievement and expecting to feel a certain way once it's accomplished. Instead, we must get clear on how we want to feel and be, *and then* choose goals that are most likely to support that quality of experience. So, when clients tell me they don't know what they want, I kindly disagree; they do.

For example, it may be important for you to be creative, challenged, financially stable, influential, peaceful, vital, and connected to your peers. These are the starting criteria to inform your career decisions so that you will be most satisfied. You know how you want to feel and be—you don't need to spend hours on LinkedIn to figure that out.

This chapter is about helping you develop the skill of clarity, knowing what's true for you. So, let's get to work. Below is the Vision Generator tool, a step-by-step approach to asking yourself the right questions to figure out what you really want. It's a simple fill-in-the-blanks exercise.

Identifying what feels good can actually be hard for some people, especially if you're the type of person who automatically puts others' needs ahead of your own. If that's the case, you may be great at assessing what your boss, mom, and partner want but less attuned to what you need in the moment because your antennae are fine-tuned to receive signals from outside of yourself. Now is your time to practice attuning to the your inner signals. You can learn how to do this, and that's what you're starting now.

From Stuck to Alive

If you don't do this inner work first, it's very likely that you'll keep experiencing more of the same feelings of stuckness. Even if you change teams, find a new job, or switch careers, you'd only shift your outer circumstances, but not necessarily adjust your inner experience. And that's why, no matter where you work, there you are. Knowing your vision helps you reorient when you get offtrack, even when you get stung by some comparison. Your vision will drag you out of stuckness into aliveness.

Your brain doesn't know the difference between reality and your vision. Having a clear vision of how you want to be isn't just inspirational; it actually has a tangible effect on your performance and even your body. Dr. Guang Yue of the Cleveland Clinic Foundation proved that you can build bigger muscles just by thinking about using them.[1]

In his experiment, Yue divided thirty healthy participants into four groups. The first group of eight was trained to perform "mental contractions" of their pinkie finger. The second group of eight participants performed mental contractions of the elbow. The third group of eight was not trained but participated in all measurements and served as a control group. Finally, the six volunteers in the fourth group physically trained their pinkie finger. All training lasted for twelve weeks (15 minutes per day, 5 days per week).

At the end, those who conducted mental training of the pinkie finger showed a 35 percent increase in strength. The group doing mental training of the elbow showed an increase in strength of 13.5 percent. Those who physically trained their finger saw an increase in strength of 53 percent. The control group showed no significant changes in strength for either finger-abduction or elbow-flexion tasks.

Wow! Just by doing mental training (and literally *not* lifting a finger), you can increase your finger's strength by 35 percent! That's because your thoughts generate similar mental instructions as real actions do. Not only that, other studies have found that doing mental exercises can improve your motivation, confidence, and chances for success in any endeavor in life.[2] So, because your brain doesn't know the difference between mental instructions and actual events, why not start imagining yourself as the person you want to be and see what happens? Ready?

Vision Generator

TOOL

Write a few sentences to fill in the blanks in the prompts below. Give yourself twenty minutes to get a first draft. You can always go back and add or edit, but there's no need to write a novel. Here's the scenario:

Imagine that you've just woken up from a deep sleep and it's five years from today. All your desires and goals have actualized. Describe what you are experiencing.

Use these ideas to help capture your vision on paper:

- Write in either the present or past tense (but not the future tense). Feel like a kid in a candy store and pick out all the candy you want. Let this delight you!

- Choose with a sense of freedom versus obligation. If images come up that feel draining or obligatory, scrap them and choose what elevates you.

(continues)

(continued)

- Capture whatever comes to mind—even if it doesn't make total sense. Approach this with playfulness and possibility. Don't judge yourself. This may feel challenging because you're not used to thinking without limitations. Some of us have been told to be "realistic," which is code for "don't dream too big." But here you have total permission to go for it. Tell the critical voice, "Thanks for trying to take care of me, but I can play around for just this exercise."

- Don't worry about choosing the perfect words or images. This doesn't have to be a literal list of activities and events in your future—this is more about uncovering how you want to *be* and *feel*. For example, if you imagine yourself doing yoga in Bali— perhaps that signals your desire for deep relaxation, ultimate freedom, or natural beauty. If you find yourself stuck because you're not sure about an answer, move on to the next prompt.

- This isn't about figuring out *how* any of this will transpire. Nor should it be limited to what you think is feasible. The goal is to capture clues about what brings you most alive. Notice what your body says. State whatever thoughts bring you joy, give you a tiny surge of energy, or help you feel lighter.

Download the electronic journal form for more space to write and stay organized. Visit www.workhappinessmethod .com/download or scan the QR code with your smartphone

▶ It's five years from now and the date and time is . . .

_____

_____

▶ I'm sitting and reflecting on my life in one of my favorite spots, which makes me feel . . .

_____

_____

▶ The top five things I love about my life and my job right now are . . .

_____

_____

▶ I'm blessed to have these people in my life . . .

_____

_____

▶ I love how I spend my time with the people in my life. For example, we . . . and it makes me feel . . .

_____

_____

▶ What's most satisfying about my romantic relationship is . . .

_____

_____

▶ Financially, things are going great. I'm grateful that . . .

_____

_____

▶ When I look back at the past five years, I appreciate how much I've grown. I'm now...

_____

_____

▶ I've transformed in so many ways. For example...

_____

_____

▶ And I've overcome these three things...

_____

_____

▶ Thinking about how I... fills me with a great sense of fulfillment and meaning.

_____

_____

▶ I finally feel content with the flow of my week. I love that...has (have) become a regular habit(s) or ritual(s) for me.

_____

_____

▶ What I appreciate most about my schedule is...

_____

_____

▶ When I wake up I feel . . . and look forward to . . .

_____

_____

▶ Finally, I get to be . . .

_____

_____

▶ What I love about the people I work/interact with is that they . . .

_____

_____

▶ The leaders I'm surrounded by are . . . and they make me feel . . .

_____

_____

▶ When working with my colleagues (or clients), I am . . .

_____

_____

▶ Every day I get to use my talent and strengths in . . .

_____

_____

▶ When it comes to the process in which I do my work, I most enjoy . . .

_____

_____

▶ I feel proud that I've accomplished these five things . . .

_____

_____

▶ I'm also recognized and appreciated in a satisfying way, for example . . .

_____

_____

▶ Before bed, when reflecting on my day, I feel good about my progress and I'm grateful that . . .

_____

_____

▶ I remember the moment when I committed to this vision. One very small thing I did five years ago that helped me realize this vision was . . .

_____

_____

Your Turn

This type of activity has optimism-boosting power. Dozens of studies have examined the effects of a best-possible-self exercise like this, and though there's still more to learn, the consensus is that generating your vision has immediate effects on your mood and gives you a brighter outlook on the future.[3] Not only that, but it can also motivate you to take better care of yourself and improve your well-being. Try it now!

If you're not feeling happier after using the Vision Generator, perhaps you're worried about how to make your vision a reality. We're getting there. The Vision Generator is not supposed to answer "What's next?" It's designed to help you plug into the person you want to be. It's what precedes goals and decisions. Deciding how to make good choices— that's coming up next in Chapter 3.

I also want to note that some people, myself included, can get agitated doing a best-possible-self exercise. If you grew up in a family that told you not to dream big, dismissed your desires, or told you to be "realistic," of course it can feel uncomfortable stretching in this way. Just notice what you notice. Don't try to love it if you don't. And be gentle with that voice that's telling you this is a waste of time. That part of you is trying to protect you.

Clarity Practice

Avoid Comparison Triggers

Are there situations you can avoid to minimize falling into the trap of comparison? If you're feeling vulnerable, why put yourself in a situation that could exacerbate insecurities? Take stock of who you surround yourself with and what information you consume. Just as we monitor what foods we put into our bodies, we also need to monitor what interactions and media we take in. I'm not saying avoid those people or quit Instagram completely. Rather, consciously expose yourself when you feel sturdy.

Write Your Vision If You Haven't Already

You can always add and edit if anything occurs to you later. This is a living, breathing document, so continue to finesse it

(continues)

(continued)

at any time. Let your vision seep in and notice whether your existing job and life reverberate with what you've written. Sometimes my clients report that they're already living their vision—what a beautiful outcome! That means less self-doubt; the vision is fortifying and a source to return to if they start to question themselves.

For others, the vision feels like an impossible dream. If that's the case for you, dig into the sensations you want to feel versus the events you describe and notice what ways you might access those sensations now. For example, if you want to be more creative at work and don't have the role you like, could you express your creativity in other ways? Savor the slivers of the desired experience you have now; coming up, we'll get into how you can have more of it.

Don't Forget to Notice What You Notice

Noticing is the ultimate way to expand the spaciousness within yourself, the place from which you make conscious decisions. We control ourselves from this place in between our thoughts.

CHAPTER 3

Purpose

How to Make Conscious Decisions with Confidence and Live Your Values Every Day

It used to take me twenty minutes to pick out cereal. I'd stand in the grocery aisle feeling like I had cement bricks strapped to my feet, stuck and slowly spiraling down into decision fatigue. My eyes would scan the nutrition labels of dozens of cardboard packages, each claiming to be the one for me. The mental calculations of weighing options—Is it better to settle for more protein and less taste? Gluten free or extra fiber?—would overwhelm me. My family and friends would get so frustrated grocery shopping with me; there would be countless eyerolls while they waited for my final call. Feeling afraid to make the wrong decision haunted me not only when it came to breakfast options but also when it came to figuring out my purpose and what the hell to do with my life, setting me up for total anguish and confusion.

And here you are. You're reading this because you're also probably struggling with a decision. Maybe it's whether to stay at your job or to go, to speak up for yourself or to keep quiet, to ask for the promotion or to wait, to acknowledge how your coworker was rude or to let it pass, again. Wherever your crossroads, you're about to create a road map that will always help you find your way Home (with a capital *H*). In other words, find your way back to your vision—that destination that brings you most alive, where you feel limitless and a deep sense of peace, where your heart swells in gratitude for the beauty of your life, and where you are consciously making progress and growing into the person you're proud to be.

Purpose

I define living on purpose as the process of finding your way Home to yourself, making one conscious choice at a time. In order to live purposefully, you need your values to guide you. Your values are the guideposts that influence the decisions you make and the actions you take moving toward your vision.[1] Your values keep you in the correct lane. Otherwise, you'd end up driving to a destination that's not of your choosing and that doesn't feel like Home. If you're not intentionally expressing your values, you'll feel inner conflict and uncertainty. Your confidence may suffer and you may start to sabotage your productivity and efforts. Instead of feeling in command of your experience, you might feel lost or easily swayed. You may question yourself or even have an identity crisis (been there, done that). Often people tell me, "Oh, I just landed here in this job. I never chose this path, I just didn't know what else to do." Sometimes you can get lucky. But, ultimately, you don't want to passively let the options lead you; instead, you want to lead your career by choosing or creating options that energize you.

The simple truth is that if you're not living in alignment with your values, you're living in alignment with someone else's—maybe your dad's, second-grade teacher's, friend's, boss's, or society's. When you develop the inner skill of purpose and know your values, you can discern between who you're told you should be, how you should act, what you should want, and what's actually true for you.

Now, you may say to yourself, "Values, shmalues. I know what my values are and I still have no idea what to do." Perhaps you've even clarified your values with a coach before. Well, this work isn't about you knowing; this work is about you being. If you're not intentionally using your values as guideposts for your choices, then let's get to work.

Of course you *know* your values—they're *yours*. You can recognize your values as easily as you can pick out your socks from a pile of clothes. But isn't it a pain in the ass to rummage through a dryer full of clean clothes just to find your favorite pair?

Have you ever done laundry for your entire family and left everything in the dryer instead of folding it and putting it away? Then, during the week when you need your special blue socks, you have to crouch down, stick your head into the dark dryer, and rummage through the entire load. Sometimes when we face a big decision and aren't sure what to do, that's what it looks like. We try to find the answer that's true for us, but we're in an uncomfortable dark place with a bunch of other people's stuff in the way. It's frustrating. And midway through the process you start beating yourself up: "Why didn't I just fold the laundry in the first place?" Or "Why hasn't someone else done this for me?! Why don't I have this figured out by now?" Well, my friend, I'm going to help you fold, sort, and put away your "laundry" so that when it comes to making a decision, you can do so easily, swiftly, and without it feeling like such a mess.

Grab a pencil.

This next exercise is called the Truth Organizer because it takes all that wisdom you have about yourself that's currently jumbled inside of you and tossed around with everyone else's stuff and tidies it up so that you can use it to live on purpose. So that you can make decisions swiftly, cool as a cucumber, because you *know* in your core that it's what's right for your flourishing. Imagine how much time you'll save and turmoil you'll avoid just by knowing how to make better decisions.

So, before we dive in, keep this in mind.

- I'm not gonna lie. This exercise requires energy and concentration. The investment you make will pay off. This exercise has directly saved my clients from losing tremendous amounts of time, money, and well-being. It's enabled them to gain a sense of purpose, increase their confidence, and achieve fulfillment. It's worth it.
- If you are feeling burned out or exhausted, be gentle with yourself and consider reading through the exercise and then returning when you're ready to do it. You may also consider partnering with a coach, mentor, or friend to support you.
- You can always do a first round to get your feet wet and then revisit it, as previously mentioned. Consider what you do now a rough draft. It will probably take you a few rounds to get the language right anyway. Getting the wording to reflect what you mean takes trial and error.
- Your values should be based on how you want to be rather than reflect the current state of affairs. You get to choose. For example, one of my values is to be organized. My husband will tell you that I'm not naturally organized. In fact, it took him years of nudging me to put the mayo back into the same place in the fridge door for me to do it. I value being organized because I know it creates ease, and I take actions daily to uphold it. I'm not always 100 percent organized, but I've gotten much better. My value has guided me closer and closer to having an Instagram-worthy T-shirt drawer. Therefore, no worries if you're not living your values now; just consider how you want to be so you can gently make your way toward becoming your vision.
- If any of this feels uncomfortable, know that it's normal and usually a signal that you're growing.

Let's get started!

If you'd like a worksheet to fill out online or to print, please visit workhappinessmethod.com/download. Or scan this QR code with your smartphone.

Truth Organizer

Step 1: Messy Brain Dump

Identify ten to fifteen desired qualities, attributes, sensations, and traits that you'd like to embody or experience at work and in life. For a head start, review your vision statement and see if any words, phrases, or ideas pop. Use those in your messy brain dump.

Here's a fictional example of Claudia's values:

Flexibility	In-Person Collaboration
Direct Communication	Mutual Respect
Transparency	Having a Seat at the Table
Financial Security	Feeling on Purpose
Clear Goals and Deadlines	Enough Energy Left Over After Work
Autonomy	Feeling Like I'm Making a Difference
Self-Care	Well-Being

Now go ahead and make your list:

Step 2: Clean Up

Review your list and consolidate where there is overlap in the underlying meaning of terms. For example, "Feeling on Purpose" and "Feeling Like I'm Making a Difference" essentially get at the same sensation of contributing to something bigger for Claudia. What you mean by each term is subjective. Just reference the underlying sensation or state that you're describing. For this example, "Transparency" and "Direct Communication" could also overlap. Claudia realizes that ultimately "Well-Being" and having "Enough Energy Left Over After Work" and space for "Self-Care" also get at the same thing for her. You may find more clarity after you define each term (next step) and after you live with these for a week or so. Don't feel pressure to combine them; I'm just offering this as a space for you to consolidate if it makes sense.

Flexibility	In-Person Collaboration
Direct Communication	Mutual Respect
~~Transparency~~	Having a Seat at the Table
Financial Security	~~Feeling on Purpose~~
Clear Goals and Deadlines	~~Enough Energy Left Over After Work~~
Autonomy	Feeling Like I'm Making a Difference
~~Self-Care~~	Well-Being

Step 3: Personalize Your Definition of Each Term

"Flexibility," for example, for one person can be defined as "working from any location." For another, "flexibility" means having the power to choose projects and clients. For someone else it can mean working part-time. Describe your ideal experience as specifically as you can. Here's what Claudia chose for her definitions.

Flexibility: I have control over my time and choose when and where I work so I can prioritize my family.	**In-Person Collaboration:** I feel supported by a team, so it's not overwhelming or lonely. This includes brainstorming formally and informally to get the best solutions.
Direct Communication: I express my truth, needs, and desires and seek out transparency with others.	**Mutual Respect:** I work in a place with people whose intellect and values I respect. Vice versa.
Financial Security: I'm able to afford a comfortable lifestyle while saving for retirement and my children's college.	**Having a Seat at the Table:** My leaders value my opinion and I contribute to the strategy of our work.
Clear Goals and Deadlines: I understand what I'm working toward and when it is due. If it's vague, I seek to make it clear.	**Feeling Like I'm Making a Difference:** My work and mentorship matter. I practice kindness and paying it forward. I seek out the meaning in my work.
Autonomy: I work with leaders who trust me to do what's best for my team and projects.	**Well-Being:** I intentionally choose to support my mental, emotional, physical, social, and spiritual health. This includes practicing healthy boundaries to create space for me to think, create, and take care of myself.

Step 4: Title Your Values

This is optional. You can leave the language as is to serve as the name of your values. Or you can make them more concise, fun, and memorable. Whatever is code for you getting into the zone you describe.

Claudia modified the following:

- "In-Person Collaboration" changes to "Supported." Ultimately, what's important is collaboration with people who help Claudia do her best work. It might not have to be in person; she just wants to feel that someone has her back.

- "Well-Being" changes to "Vitality" because it just pops more and sings with the vibe of feeling bright and alive.
- "Feeling Like I'm Making a Difference" changes to "Service Leadership" because it's a more direct way for Claudia to remember that making a difference means catapulting others and doing what's best for the people and organization.
- "Mutual Respect" changes to "R-E-S-P-E-C-T" because Claudia loves the tune and it's fun to plug into Aretha Franklin.

Step 5: Rank Your Values

Inevitably, at some point your values will conflict and you'll be standing at a fork in the road unsure which path is right. You have to choose which value is more important. Ranking them today will make life easier tomorrow when they conflict.

Claudia might confront a dilemma in which a project will give her the opportunity to experience more Service Leadership but at the expense of Vitality. Both of those values are important to her, but Claudia is burned out and has been putting her well-being on the back burner for years. She knows that it now has to be her top priority. She can't afford to take on any projects that would compromise her health, so she prioritizes Vitality over Service Leadership.

Ranking can feel challenging. You'll get to test out your results in the real world and modify if necessary. The intention here is to make complex decisions simpler. Ranking is a grand gesture of self-care. You're supporting your future self by getting quiet and thoughtful now. Usually, your values stay consistent over time, but how you rank them changes based on your circumstances. Here's how Claudia ranks her values:

1. **Vitality:** I intentionally choose to support my mental, emotional, physical, social, and spiritual health. This includes practicing healthy boundaries to create space for me to think, create, and take care of myself.

2. **Flexibility:** I have control over my time and choose when and where I work so I can prioritize my family.

3. **Service Leadership:** My work and mentorship matter. I prioritize people and their growth versus my ego.

4. **Direct Communication:** I express my truth, needs, and desires and seek out transparency with others.

5. **Supported:** I feel supported by a team, so it's not overwhelming or lonely. This includes brainstorming formally and informally to get the best solutions.

6. **R-E-S-P-E-C-T:** I work in a place with people whose intellect and values I respect. Vice versa.

7. **Having a Seat at the Table:** My leaders value my opinion, and I contribute to the strategy of our work.

8. **Financial Security:** I'm able to afford a comfortable lifestyle while saving for retirement and my children's college.

9. **Clear Goals and Deadlines:** I understand what I'm working toward and when it is due. If it's vague, I seek to make it clear.

10. **Autonomy:** I work with leaders who trust me to do what's best for my team and projects.

Step 5.5: Feel Free to Modify, Edit, Delete, or Add Values Here If You're Missing Any

Skip this if you're feeling good about your list now. In this example, Claudia realizes, "Hmm, Flexibility and Autonomy feel like they're getting at the same thing for me." She decides to collapse them into one and modify the definition:

> **Autonomy:** I have control over my time and choose when and where I work so I can prioritize my family. My leaders trust me to do what's best for my team and projects.

The gist is that you can always examine and adjust along the way, even in a few days, months, or years.

Step 6: Rate Yourself

Assess to what degree you are experiencing each value now on a scale from 0 to 100 percent. This will help you see where you stand and where you can amplify your experience of a value.

Don't worry if you get some really low scores. This is just a data point to inform you of where you might want to apply more focus. If you put your attention on amplifying a value, you will see your experience of it improve. Many clients notice improvements within four to eight weeks.

Here are Claudia's scores:

1. Vitality	50%
2. Autonomy	85%
3. Service Leadership	70%
4. Direct Communication	30%
5. Supported	40%
6. R-E-S-P-E-C-T	70%
7. Having a Seat at the Table	60%
8. Financial Security	80%
9. Clear Goals and Deadlines	15%

Step 7: Identify Three Values to Focus on Improving over the Next Three Months

I ask you to focus on three for the time being because there's only so much you can track. You can reevaluate after three months. You don't have to automatically choose the values that have the lowest scores. I suggest you set a calendar reminder to reflect on whether you want to update your chosen three.

Here is Claudia's focus:

Vitality: I intentionally choose to support my mental, emotional, physical, social, and spiritual health. This includes practicing healthy boundaries to create space for me to think, create, and take care of myself.

Service Leadership: My work and mentorship matter. I prioritize people and their growth versus my ego.

Supported: I feel supported by a team, so it's not overwhelming or lonely. This includes brainstorming formally and informally to get the best solutions.

My three chosen focus values are:

1. _____

2. _____

3. _____

Accountability Questions

TOOL

Accountability questions are a way for you to check in on how you're actively living each of the three values you selected in Step 7. Don't worry, answering your accountability questions each day only takes about two minutes. But the impact is *huge*.

Your accountability questions should be open ended and prevent a yes/no response. For example, instead of *"Did* I appreciate my team today?" ask, *"How* did I express appreciation to my team?" The latter extracts more inquiry and nudges you to find an answer. The former cuts off reflection and leads to a quick yes or no response.

(continues)

(continued)

Here are more examples of open-ended accountability questions:

- How did I express love and affection for my family?
- In what ways did I take action to generate revenue?
- What bold actions did I take today?
- How did I exercise control over my negative thinking today?
- How did I speak my truth today?
- When did I listen to my body today?
- How did I express my creativity today?
- How did I practice being kind?
- In what ways was I playful today?

Claudia's accountability questions are:

- **Vitality:** What did I do to support my well-being today?
- **Service Leadership:** How did I provide mentorship or support to my team?
- **Supported:** In what ways did I delegate effectively or create conditions for collaboration?

My accountability questions are:

1. _____

2. _____

3. _____

I encourage my clients to add a fourth question: How can I do better tomorrow? Because some days will just fly by and you'll forget. We're all human! And one more: What am I grateful for? Let's just roll in the gratitude for the daily practice! All optional—but thought I'd squeeze them in there for you.

Resistance to Answering Accountability Questions

Let's discuss why it's *so* important to reflect on your accountability questions daily. Progress, motivation, confidence, oh my! Most over-achievers forget to recognize their progress, and this leaves them with a constant feeling of being behind or overwhelmed by a never-ending to-do list. Can you relate? Do you feel like there's never enough time in the day? Or maybe you don't have enough energy to do everything you want to do?

Researchers Teresa Amabile and Steven Kramer conducted rigorous analysis of twelve thousand diary entries provided by hundreds of employees and discovered that acknowledging progress was the most important driver of employees' emotions and motivation at work—beyond recognition, incentives, and support.[2] They call this the "progress principle." They found that everyday progress, even a small win, could make all the difference in how an employee experienced their work and themselves. In fact, when participants described having "the best day," it was triggered by making progress in their work.

But if you're always on the go in back-to-back meetings, it's easy to forget or overlook your wins. That's why I intentionally kick off each coaching call by asking my clients to celebrate their progress. James, a senior director of a consumer goods company, is a great example of this. He was frustrated that he hadn't been promoted to vice president yet. Each time he'd bring it up with his manager, he'd leave the meeting without any sense of what else he could do to improve or how long he'd have to wait. He felt ignored and stuck. When we started our coaching call one day, he admitted that he didn't have much to celebrate that week. Thirty minutes later he said in passing, "Oh, yeah, I forgot to mention... my boss said the CEO is giving me an opportunity to lead a new project to groom me into VP material."

"WHAT! James, this is HUGE!" I exclaimed.

We spent time celebrating this major milestone in his growth and what excited him about this move. He left the call feeling massively more energized and accomplished. All we did was create some space for James to remember, acknowledge, and appreciate what happened. That's the simple but profound role these accountability questions will play for you.

By having awareness of your values, making aligned choices, and then acknowledging your progress, you engage in what I call a Virtuous Trifecta. The more you practice using your accountability questions, the more motivated you become to make better decisions.

VIRTUOUS TRIFECTA

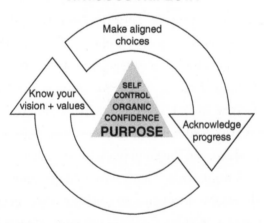

This is living on purpose. And this is what gives way to organic confidence.

Organic Confidence

Organic confidence results from witnessing yourself take control over your reality. It's when you feel comfortable in your power and are in command of yourself. You know you have influence over your reality and consciously use it. You make decisions with clarity and intention. Organic confidence supports you in communicating in a way that's effective and compassionate (more on that in Chapter 6).

When you answer your accountability questions at the end of the day, they help you feel a sense of achievement, completion, and closure so you can relax and go to bed with peace in your heart, knowing you made today matter.

When it comes to your responses, beware that on certain days your inner critic will judge your progress as not enough. But this isn't about measuring *how much* progress you made; the intention of asking your accountability questions is to give yourself credit for *any* progress. Even if you accidentally took action in alignment with your values without knowing it, you still win.

Researchers Joseph Nunes and Xavier Drèze conducted a study at a car wash, where they found we can trick ourselves into making progress by pretending we've already made some.[3] The study provided three hundred customers with a loyalty card. Half of the customers were issued a loyalty card with spaces for eight stamps, the deal being that they'd get a free car wash after the eighth stamp. The other half of the customers received a card with space for ten stamps, and two of the stamps were already affixed. Although both groups had to purchase the same number of car washes to get the reward, the second group's card implied that they were one-fifth of the way there. In nine months, 19 percent of the eight-stamp-card group received a free car wash and 32 percent of the ten-stamp-card group received a free car wash. The authors call this the *endowed progress effect*, whereby people are more likely to persist with a goal if they're provided artificial advancement. Your accountability questions provide you with real advancement. But even if your inner critic doesn't think that's enough, just know that acknowledging any progress is working on giving you a boost to keep going.

So, in conclusion, accountability questions help you:

- acknowledge your progress, which helps you
- stay motivated, which helps you
- make decisions that are more values based, which helps you
- shape your reality into your own vision, which helps you
- develop organic confidence, which helps you
- realize how powerful you are, which helps you
- live on purpose no matter what you're dealing with or with whom

Please, give yourself credit. Do your accountability questions! Just a few minutes of reflection can change your day and even your destiny. I can't emphasize enough how important it is to know your values and use them...but let me try.

Step 8: Develop Values-Based (Small) Goals

When you know your values, you're empowered to take charge of your career fulfillment by setting goals and making decisions that really matter to you. Let's imagine Claudia's situation. She scored herself as 40 percent on her Service Leadership value. I'd ask Claudia, "If you want to nudge your score from 40 percent to 50 percent, what's one small thing you could do this week?" Immediately, a number of simple options would emerge. For example, she could:

- Set up one-on-one meetings with each team member to check in about their career goals
- Gather her team for lunch to reconnect
- Make it a point on their status calls to appreciate the team's efforts
- Read a book on service leadership

What are small steps you can take immediately to express your values more, even by 10 percent? I like to start small so you can generate fast wins and gather evidence that things can change. Take a moment now to brainstorm the many ways you could do this. You should notice there are tiny actions you can take right now, without asking for permission. Write down your specific ideas.

▶ Three small things I can do to live my value of _____ :

1. _____

2. _____

3. _____

Is It You? Or the Job?

If you're struggling at work, clarifying your values helps you understand whether it's you or your job that needs to shift. It's common to question whether you're in the right place and if you're doing enough to grow. Once you've organized your values, ranked and rated them, you have a system for deciding.

I've worked with dozens of clients who were spinning their wheels only to finally realize, "Oh, I'm actually in a good place. I can just focus on doing my job instead of worrying about what's next." How wonderful to feel at peace and be able to relax! Imagine how much more resourced you'll feel if all that anxiety you had about what's next was contained. I've also worked with clients who gained enough clarity to see that their current position and conditions weren't sustainable. This gave them the confidence to explore possibilities that better aligned with their values.

If You're Willing to Quit, You Have the Option to Be Brave

Before you start searching for new opportunities, do your best to improve your scores to get more aligned with your values. That way you can be certain you did your part. I often tell my clients when they're on the verge of quitting that this is an exciting opportunity for them to use their current job as a laboratory for their professional (or, heck, personal) development. Why not ask to work on the project you've been coveting, have the difficult conversation with your boss that you've been avoiding, practice saying no, or finally learn how to delegate better? Play and explore ways to bolster those values. You can always leave if nothing changes or if it's too hard to be who you want to be at this job. But, in the meanwhile, you'll have grown by trying. By the way, we're going to cover boundaries next and difficult conversations in Chapter 7.

Use Your Values to Shape Your Career Development Conversations

Leaders love when employees do the Work Happiness Method because then professional development conversations are more rich with possibilities. You come to the table with greater clarity. My client David was a UX researcher who was eager to take his career to the next level. Although he was scoring about 80–95 percent on four of his top values, when it came to "Growth," his number one value, he was at 30 percent. He told his manager that he was working with a coach and that, though he loved his role and his group, he needed a greater sense of challenge. David's manager immediately came up with an idea for David to work on a new team that was being assembled. Had David not informed his boss of his values, his manager would have never connected the dots and recommended David for this new position. Take a moment to consider which aspects of your values you can share with your boss to have better career development conversations.

Sharing Your Values Can Help Your Team Work Better Together

My client Connie has a value of "Connection" that manifests as discussing and generating ideas aloud. She happens to work with introverts who prefer not to talk through as much as she does. With clarity around her values, Connie was able to articulate her needs: "Hey, guys, I've realized that in order for me to feel connected and plugged in and to do my best work, I'd like us to brainstorm aloud together before we move to the next phase. Can we build this into our process?" By framing her need for verbal processing together as part of her values and what she needs to thrive, she shifted the tone of her group. They went from being slightly annoyed to formally embracing Connie's ideation style. It was a win-win because the team formed boundaries around when Connie would ideate aloud and Connie formalized space for her to brainstorm.

Now that you have a road map of what's important to you, how can you better communicate the conditions you need to those around you? As in Connie's situation, sharing your values isn't just about getting your needs met but also about supporting your team members. Don't be fooled in thinking that expressing your needs is selfish. When you create conditions to thrive, you are enabling yourself to be of greatest service to your team and organization. You become a pleasure to be around. You add way more value. And your family and friends probably prefer you when you're less grumpy. That said, the only disclaimer here is that your fulfillment and happiness at work can't override tending to your responsibilities.

Knowing Your Values Protects You from Imposter Syndrome

First described by psychologists Suzanne Imes and Pauline Rose Clance, imposter syndrome occurs among high achievers who are unable to internalize and accept their success.[4] It's when you think, "Oh, I'm only in this position because I got lucky." When you feel like an imposter, you worry about being exposed as a fraud. You feel like you don't deserve your position or accolades.

But if you're doing your accountability questions and demonstrating to yourself how you're making conscious decisions that lead to being the professional and person you aspire to be, you make it difficult to assign responsibility for your growth to just plain luck. Participating in the Virtuous Trifecta—having awareness of your values, making aligned choices, and acknowledging your progress—reminds you of how much control you have. You witness your agency. And when that happens, you embody confidence.

Purpose Practice

Practice your accountability questions every day (or as often as you can). It should only take you two or three minutes. I recommend jotting down your answers for at least the first month of practice because writing makes your progress more tangible. You can use a journal or download worksheets I've created for you at workhappinessmethod .com/download. Or scan the QR code with your smartphone.

► Go ahead and answer your accountability questions for today.

1. _____

_____

_____

2. _____

_____

_____

3. _____

_____

_____

▶ Bonus: How can I do better tomorrow?

_____

_____

▶ Bonus: What am I grateful for today?

_____

_____

▶ One small way I will express my values more deeply this next week is to:

_____

_____

CHAPTER 4

Boundaries

How to Self-Care and Avoid Burnout

I used to be a welcome mat, listening to anyone's problems and going out of my way to help them. Instead of relaxing during a massage, I'd tend to my massage therapist, who was complaining about his boss. Instead of being supported by vendors, I'd do half their work for them. Instead of leaving a bad relationship, I agreed to get engaged (I canceled it in time, by the way). Of course, having empathy is a virtue, even a superpower, but without healthy boundaries, it's toxic. And not just toxic for you but also for those you think you're helping. It confuses things. Sometimes people don't know that they're overriding your boundaries, so by not enforcing those boundaries, you're just enabling their bad behavior or burning yourself out.

Boundaries Aren't Just About Saying No

In fact, boundaries are about saying yes to what's important.

I define a boundary as a conscious agreement that you set with yourself to support your needs and make your life more comfortable.

Boundaries enable you to better express your values and operate with greater freedom, security, and ease. I say it's a *conscious agreement* because conflicting parts of yourself have to come together and resolve what takes priority.

My therapist encourages me to have a board meeting with different parts of myself when I'm resisting a boundary. For example, to finish writing this chapter I chose to seclude myself at a friend's empty house in upstate New York. I was conflicted and ready to back out last minute. Instead, I chose to conference with the different parts of myself. The mom in me felt obligated to be there for my kids when they got home. The wife in me felt guilty for asking my husband to solo parent, even though he was totally supportive. The writer in me was desperate to get away and have space to think and breathe. I acknowledged the sense of duty and guilt, and I also noticed the writer, who was starting to feel resentful. The writer had taken a back seat and was now putting her foot down and saying, "This is my time. This is a dream of mine and I'm saying *yes* to it and *no* to the family obligations...for a few days."

Acknowledging all the feelings and parts of me was helpful in easing my resistance and aligning around my decision to go. It's not easy to sort out and detangle mixed emotions, obligations, and desires. That's why doing your vision and values before you tackle boundaries is beneficial. When you find yourself torn or unsure of what to do, lean on your vision and values to spotlight your *yes*, and move toward that. Journal what the voices have to say and then choose on the basis of what lines up with your integrity, not fear.

On to you. Have you ever found yourself being too nice, too accommodating, or too understanding? If so, have you thought about what it's costing you? When we automatically put other people's needs ahead of our own, it's likely we're tolerating draining and potentially harmful experiences. They can be light tolerances, such as putting up with a messy office or answering emails into the night. Or they might be more intense, such as accepting abusive behavior at work. Of course, being kind and helpful are virtues, but not if they're hurting you.

Take a moment to scan a typical day and reflect on what you're tolerating and what it's costing you. Examples of costs include time, money, growth opportunities, or emotional/social/physical well-being.

▶ I'm tolerating_____.

    It's costing me _____.

▶ I'm tolerating_____.

    It's costing me _____.

▶ I'm tolerating_____.

    It's costing me _____.

Tolerating experiences for the sake of being agreeable can be an indicator it's time to set some boundaries. Not sure about your boundary health? Here are some additional signals that can identify whether your boundaries need reinforcement. See if any of them resonate.

Do you...

- hate inconveniencing others?
- obsessively worry about hurting other people's feelings?
- take over other people's tasks because they can't manage to do them right?
- say yes to things you later regret agreeing to?

- feel resentful because you're giving, giving, giving and not receiving in return?
- feel guilty when you do anything for yourself?
- avoid certain people because you don't have it in you to say no?
- have a hard time knowing how you feel or what you need in the moment?
- feel overwhelmed and burned out?
- consistently work past your limit?

I've checked every aforementioned box. When I think back to the many ways I've abandoned myself out of a compulsive desire to make people happy, it's hard not to wince. But knowing the origin story of how I got this way has helped me develop self-compassion and motivated me to develop healthy boundaries. I've learned that although it's not my fault that I became this way, it is my responsibility to do something about it. That's the theme of all this work—you are a wonderful, whole, innocent, complete being to whom life has happened. You live in a system that is not fair or perfect. But this doesn't mean that your past or the system determines who you are. You do have a choice. It takes work. For some, it takes a lot more.

I'll share my story and distill years of therapy into a few paragraphs. I offer this to illuminate why boundaries are a struggle for me (which may not be your experience at all). Let's start with a quick PSYC 101 to set it up.

Fawning and How Trauma Affects Boundary Setting

You've heard of the fight-or-flight response to stress, right? Well, we have two additional responses to threat: A third response is called "freeze or faint," which is when you lose control of your body; you might feel cold, numb, heavy, or stiff; and you have trouble moving, your breath slows down, and you experience a sense of dread. A fourth response—the one primarily associated with poor boundaries—is called *fawning*, a term coined by Pete Walker, a psychotherapist who wrote *Complex PTSD: From Surviving to Thriving.*[1]

People who fawn, or "fawners," repress their feelings, thoughts, and needs in order to appease others.[2] On the outside, fawners may seem as if they are perfectly fine, but on the inside they are disassociating from themselves. Most of their energy is focused on others, they're hyperaware of other people's emotions and needs, and they prioritize those over their own in order to avoid danger, real or perceived. This is why it's difficult for fawners to even know what they want in the moment. Fawners are overly agreeable and polite. They will go along with others' perspectives, beliefs, or values almost automatically. They avoid saying no. Basically, everything I described earlier that signals a need for better boundaries is embodied by fawners.

In my personal life and in work with clients, I see the tendency toward fawning as a leading culprit of poor boundaries. In many ways, fawning has helped people become successful; it's helped me. Because fawners want to please, they also tend to be perfectionists, and such tendencies tend to be rewarded in the workplace but can cost you down the line.

Fawning can develop in childhood as a means to stay attached to a parent who is stressed, neglectful, or abusive. *Attachment* refers to the closeness and affection a child feels for their main caregiver. Attachment is everything. From a primal perspective, without attachment, your survival is at risk. It's not like a baby can feed and fend for itself, right? But more than just basic needs, attachment provides a secure base for a child to explore, learn, relate, and adapt to the world around them.[3] If a child's environment is unsafe or unstable, fawning can become an adaptive coping mechanism. Studies have found that attachment begins in utero; even infants will modify their behaviors and needs in order to form attachments.[4]

My nervous system learned to keep my emotions at bay in order to keep things peaceful at home. I was an easy child in part because life got hard. My parents were refugees from Ukraine. When I was six, my father died from lung cancer and my mom was left with me, the house, and the small business they had just gotten off the ground. Being a good girl was my way of staying attached to a parent who clearly had a lot to manage. This worked out well for me until it didn't. My bouts of burnout and people-pleasing probably stem from my childhood. At least this is the story I've cobbled together with my therapist to explain my fawning behavior.

A specific traumatic experience isn't a prerequisite for fawning or poor boundaries. Just living in a culture that makes it unsafe to be unhappy can do the job. *Stop crying*, *get over it*, *buck up*, and *smile* are phrases thrown at children (and adults!) because people feel uncomfortable with other people's discomfort or difficult emotions. It can be triggering when a kid is upset, angry, or sad or having a tantrum. I'm a mom of a seven-year-old and a toddler as I write, and I'm speaking from my experience just this morning. It's hard when my kids whine or cry—it feels like my body is getting tiny electric shocks with each nag. Many adults unknowingly encourage children to override their feelings. I'm not blaming parents—who are doing the best with what they have. But when we override or numb our feelings, we disconnect from our needs. And when we're disconnected from our needs, it's more difficult to make decisions that support our well-being, happiness, and success. That's why people pleasers are at risk for burnout. They've silenced parts of themselves and just don't hear the warning signs.

Fawning is not a weakness. In fact, according to Stephen Porges, author of *The Polyvagal Theory*, fawning "comes out of a very resilient nervous system. It's not available to everyone who is in...difficult situations....It's a valiant attempt that a person's nervous system has made which enabled them to navigate this very complex world."[5] It is a superpower in many ways. I'm like a finely tuned, extra-sensitive emotional instrument. Boundaries, when I use them, help me skillfully play that instrument for good—as a coach, parent, or friend.

Burnout

According to Gallup, one in three employees is "always" or "very often" burned out.[6] The World Health Organization has classified burnout as a syndrome with three chronic symptoms:

1. *Exhaustion:* You're emotionally and physically worn out, depleted, fatigued, and even debilitated. People who are burned out are 63 percent more likely to take a sick day and 23 percent more likely to visit the emergency room.[7]

2. *Cynicism:* Your attitude toward others and your work has become negative. You may feel irritable, withdrawn, and jaded. Overachievers who are super engaged find this shift demoralizing. I remember when I had my first bout of burnout working in advertising. I went from being a go-getter who was super-motivated to barely doing my required work—quiet quitting, as they call it nowadays—or doing the bare minimum. Not being excited about anything was depressing. I couldn't recognize myself. This is why folks who are burned out are three times more likely to actually quit than those who aren't.[8]

3. *Inefficacy:* You aren't as productive and motivated as you used to be, nor do you feel as capable. Your morale is low and you have a hard time coping with challenges. Even if on the outside it looks like you're keeping up, on the inside you know how much harder it feels to do what you used to do. Which can bring up feelings of shame. This is why folks who are burned out are 50 percent less likely to discuss their goals with their manager.[9] Instead of reaching out for help, when you're burned

out you start to isolate and hide. Cue the imposter syndrome. You may start to question whether you even deserve your position or belong in your organization.

What Causes Burnout

One simple framework that explains how burnout occurs at work is called the job demands-resources model.[10] Burnout happens when you have too many demands and not enough resources. Demands are anything that deplete your energy, such as conflict, too much responsibility, and lack of support. Resources are anything that boost your energy, including quality relationships, regular feedback, and meaningful work. Burnout doesn't just happen after pulling a few all-nighters; it's a slow drip that happens over time. If you're a people pleaser who just tells yourself you can tolerate a bit more—it's easy to miss the escalating imbalance between your demands and resources.

Let's pause for a moment to reflect on your demands and your resources. What drains you? What energizes you? To consider where to set boundaries, delegate, or change any aspects of your role, I like to start by taking stock. Just as people track their spending habits when they want to start saving or track their eating when they want to change their diet, we have to track your activities and interactions to see how you spend your day.

Track Your Energy

It's important to know how you spend your energy, even on the tiny stuff. Use the following Energy Inventory Tracker to log your tasks over the week to get a realistic sense of your experience.

Itemize your activities throughout the day and then rate how you energetically respond to them on a scale of 1 to 10. Do this chronologically so you can also spot patterns, inefficiencies, multitasking, and so forth. I like doing this in an Excel worksheet so I can then sort by energy and importance and see what rises to the top. If you'd like the electronic template to log an entire week or beyond, grab it as part of the download journal at workhappinessmethod.com/download. Or scan the QR code with your smartphone.

You can also just use some paper. It's best to log in real time for at least three days, ideally a week.

In the Energy column, a score of 1 represents a task that is extremely draining. A score of 10 means you love the task and are excited by it. The Importance column helps you assess how the task relates to your responsibilities: 1 = this is not part of your job; 10 = this is one of your main responsibilities. There's also a column for observations where you can make notes. Depending on how fancy you want to get, you can plot your scores on a grid to see where you need boundaries and to potentially adjust your role.

Task	Duration (minutes)	Energy (1 = Draining, 10 = Exciting)	Importance (1 = Low, 10 = High)	Observations
Answered emails	20	2	8	Starting my day by answering emails is depleting.
Completed sales proposal for Microsoft	75	7	10	This took longer than I thought.
Scheduled meeting with Hilary's team	10	1	1	Bjorn was going to do it, but I offered.
Grabbed coffee with new interns	30	8	1	Loved their optimism and enjoyed mentoring.

Task	Duration (minutes)	Energy (1 = Draining, 10 = Exciting)	Importance (1 = Low, 10 = High)	Observations
Status update on campaign launch	60	5	10	I wonder if I can create a template so others can fill this in and it's not all on me.
Helped Rodrigo deal with team drama	45	8	3	I love helping people with people problems.
Presented plan to clients	60	10	10	Love presenting.
Research meeting	30	3	3	They don't need me there.
Brainstormed marketing ideas	120	8	8	I wish I could do this more.

ENERGY AUDIT

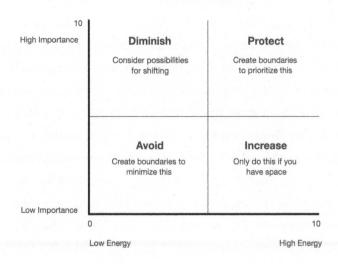

If something is high energy and high importance use boundaries to maximize that activity. If something is low energy and low importance, use boundaries to minimize that activity. If something is low energy but has high importance, reflect on it. How might you make the task more engaging? Can you delegate? Is it worth exploring with your boss? You can't ignore responsibilities just because they don't feel good. But you can consider how to re-relate to them or adjust them. If something has high energy and low importance, indulge in it if you have space. In Chapter 6, we'll talk about how to modify your role to be even more energizing. So stay tuned for more on that.

In a minute, I'll walk you through a framework on how to set healthy boundaries. But, first, I want to further emphasize just how important it is that you're willing to listen to your emotions and pay attention to your body.

Beyond Burnout: The Chronic Dangers of People-Pleasing

In his book *When the Body Says No: Exploring the Stress-Disease Connection*, Dr. Gabor Maté makes the case that people-pleasing can be quite dangerous.[11] Beyond putting you at risk for burnout, it can lead to chronic disease and death. He reveals how personality traits that we normally admire in our society and especially in the workplace can be the sources of illness: for example, go-getters with relentless drive who show up no matter what. Or overly nice employees who aim to please despite what their body is saying. Or hyperfocused employees who don't show any signs of emotion at work. Maté shares numerous studies to illustrate the connection between stress and disease. In one study, fifty-six women admitted for a breast biopsy were interviewed the day prior to their operation. They were asked questions about their upbringing and psychological state. On the basis of those answers alone, researchers were able to predict the correct diagnosis in up to 94 percent of patients who did have breast cancer and who had reported emotional repression, disconnection from parents during childhood, and compulsive caregiving.[12] In another study, Dr. David Kissen, a British chest surgeon, found that the risk of lung cancer is five times higher in men who lacked the ability to express their emotions effectively.[13] Not only do our emotions affect our mood, as I laid out in Chapter 1, but they also affect our bodies— including our nervous system, hormonal system, and ultimately our immune system. This is why developing inner skills such as emotional regulation and, in particular, boundary setting is critical—not just for your success and mental well-being but also for your physical health. This is about longevity and life and death.

Each cell in the body has a cell wall, a boundary around itself that maintains homeostasis and keeps out the bad and lets in the good. Your body is built to maintain a delicate balance to keep all systems running smoothly. But somehow, when it comes to living our lives and doing our work, we have lost touch with that natural intelligence. Boundaries support our optimal functioning by supporting our balance. We want to learn to set boundaries so that we have more ease and well-being. Boundaries help reduce stress so that we can hear ourselves and be ourselves.

The Mechanics of Stress

Let's dip into the mechanics of stress for just a sec. Stress is a response to a perceived threat to one's existence or well-being; it's a destabilization of the body's homeostasis. When stressed, your body's nervous system shifts from a parasympathetic state, rest and digest mode, to a sympathetic state, fight, flight, freeze, or fawn mode. It begins with an activating event, a stressor, which can be physical, emotional, chemical, or biological. Maybe someone cut you off in traffic, made a snide comment in a meeting, or you're just hungry. The stressor doesn't even have to be real. It can be imagined. It can be your envisioning a tough conversation and seeing the worst-case scenario. Remember, your brain doesn't know the difference between mental instructions and real events. Once your brain labels the event as a stressor and perceives a threat, it then triggers a stress response. A stress response is a series of physiological events in the body, involving the brain, the hormonal apparatus, the immune system, and many other organs. In the case of fight or flight, your adrenal glands release the stress hormones adrenaline and cortisol. This helps your body boost energy to get ready to face the potential danger or flee. To focus the body's resources, your digestion slows down, pupils dilate, heart pumps faster, breathing quickens, and muscles may even tremble. Ideally, once you're safe, you complete the stress cycle, which means your body shifts back into homeostasis and the parasympathetic mode turns on. This marks the end of that particular stress response. The problem is that, in our modern society, our bodies fail to receive the signal that we're safe, so they don't end the stress response. That's how we end up in chronic stress.

In their book *Burnout: The Secret to Unlocking the Stress Cycle*, coauthors Emily Nagoski and Amelia Nagoski discuss how eliminating the stressor doesn't mean you have eliminated the stress response itself.[14] We mistakenly believe that once we're done with the big launch, the push for a promotion, the search for a new job, or the getting-to-know-you period with a new boss we should feel okay, safe. We expect our body to follow suit. But sometimes our body doesn't get the memo that everything is okay. Our body needs to get the message through physical means, not just mental ones. Activities that help send the signal are the very ones we reviewed in Chapter 1 that help you build resilience. You know them. They work. They include sleep, exercise, walks in nature, deep breathing, a long hug, and connecting with another person. These simple physical activities, the Boring Basics, signal to your body that it's okay to relax and withdraw the stress juice pumping through your veins.

Self-Care Versus Self-Soothing

The physical activities of the Boring Basics are all examples of self-care activities, not to be confused with self-soothing actions. Self-soothing activities help you escape your reality and tune out. Which is needed in moderation—I'm all for a little Netflix marathon or glass of wine. But when you overindulge, you get that icky, hungover feeling—and those same escape activities can backfire and deplete you.

Ultimately, you need to know how to tune in and stay within your reality. That's what self-care activities do. They resource you and give you the energy to face the challenges at hand. They resource you by metabolizing your stress. They might not feel pleasurable in the moment, but they do you some good.

Stress Is Not the Enemy

The good news is that you can have a highly demanding job and life and not get burned out. The key is to resource yourself appropriately. Although you can't always control the workload or the support you get or who is on your team or even how much money you earn, you can develop inner skills to bolster your resources. The goal is not to eliminate all stress but to have the conditioning and conditions in place to deal with it. In fact, a little stress is good for you. For example, when you stress your muscles during exercise by lifting heavy weights, you encourage them to grow. But if you've never lifted weights, you don't start by doing fifty-pound biceps curls. Similarly, a project deadline can give you supportive pressure to keep moving. But unreasonable deadlines can lead to panic. The focus on boundaries is to prevent you from overdoing it and hurting yourself. Boundaries, in and of themselves, are a form of self-care—they help you keep demands in check and amplify the resources that fuel you. See boundaries less as a fence to keep things out and more as fertilizer to grow into what you want.

Jenna Never Thought She'd Be Able to Set Boundaries

For Jenna, a director of project management at a design company, boundaries felt impossible. Jenna values being of service to her team and likes being the "go to" person for anything her colleagues need, big or small. But this started to cost her. She hired me as her coach because she felt depleted and began resenting the job she once loved. At home, Jenna was easily frustrated and cranky with her children. At work, she was overwhelmed and hopeless, worried about the growing heap of projects on her plate. I asked Jenna to use the Energy Inventory Tracker and take stock of her tasks. She quickly noticed that she was spending a lot of her time on random support requests from people outside of her team instead of focusing on her actual role. Though she knew this to some degree already, seeing the hours of distraction on paper made an impression. This helped her realize that it wasn't her job that was the problem; it was her lack of boundaries.

Despite this recognition, Jenna initially resisted setting boundaries and saying no because she felt like it went against her core desire to be the go-to person. She felt conflicted. For example, why not help Amy with her report? It would only take Jenna ten minutes and save Amy hours of time. Jenna feels good when she shows up for others—so, what's the harm?

I dug into understanding why being the go-to person was important for Jenna. She told me that it came down to her desire to feel needed. Being needed meant she was valued. I then asked Jenna, if she could choose how to best serve her organization and contribute value, what would it look like? She described high-impact contributions such as excelling on her personal projects, mentoring her team, and creating space to be more strategic. It clicked for Jenna; her aha! moment finally gave her permission to practice boundaries. She realized that she could make herself even more valuable and needed by saying no to requests that didn't leverage her strengths and that distracted her. It seems so obvious, but not when you're in it. As an aside, new leaders often fall into this trap of busying themselves with tasks they feel comfortable achieving versus stretching into the higher-level responsibilities that involve talent development and planning.

Jenna and I started with baby steps. We set up a gentle experiment. Her homework over the week was to say no to one request that was outside of her scope. Jenna seized the moment when a security guard called for help. There was a vendor at the reception desk and the security guard didn't know where to send them. Because Jenna is friendly, in the know, and always makes herself available, he rang her desk. Normally, Jenna would have gone down to reception, reached out to a few people, and figured it out. This time she said, "I'm sorry, I can't help you with this. Moving forward, if you need help using the directory or figuring out who to call, here are a few ways you can do it on your own." She saved herself from a distraction that could easily have taken twenty minutes. She felt guilty afterward and regretted it immediately. (Feeling remorseful is normal and part of the process; more on that shortly.) The security guard continued to be just as friendly with Jenna, but she noticed that he stopped calling with random requests. That small win encouraged her to take more baby steps.

In six weeks her boss observed her progress and the impact she was having with her team. Jenna shared that she was working with an executive coach and being intentional about her time management. He asked her about her goals, and that led to a conversation about an unexpected promotion. He also offered his support to reinforce Jenna's new boundaries, putting her further at ease. Jenna told me that she would have turned down the promotion if she hadn't had this practice of setting boundaries. In fact, she might have even quit. But now she was authentically excited to grow and take on more. She actually had capacity and felt reinvigorated.

What Jenna learned is that when you take care of yourself, you actually end up taking better care of everyone else. Her organization benefited, her husband became my biggest fan (he got his wife back), and her kids were more relaxed around her. In an ironic twist, the best way to people please is to actually set healthy boundaries. People-pleasing without boundaries is like handing out cheap candy to hangry kids. Setting healthy boundaries is like serving a Thanksgiving Day feast and sitting down together to enjoy the warmth and abundance of the season. Ultimately, everyone is more satisfied. But it does require more effort, and it doesn't mean that there aren't bumps in the road. If you're worried about disappointing your team or your boss, imagine how much more disappointed they'd be if you quit or burned out so badly that you checked out. There may be some discomfort, but you can handle it and so can they.

Feeling Guilty Doesn't Mean It's Wrong

It's not easy to set boundaries, and if you're not used to it, you'll most likely feel guilty or remorseful. Just because you feel bad doesn't mean that it's wrong. If your nervous system is conditioned to feel safe when everyone else is pleased, of course this will feel off. You've spent a lifetime behaving one way; it will feel weird to be another way. But it doesn't mean your boundary is bad, just that you're doing something different. It may take time for you to develop new circuitry, a new path within yourself. In fact, when I notice guilt surfacing, I take that as a sign that I'm headed in the right direction. I'm working against the grain of my conditioning and making a conscious choice. It will take time and repetition to relax into it.

You have your whole life to master this skill, so please be patient with yourself. I tell myself regularly that I'm learning and that I get years and years of opportunities to practice this skill. Consider how you can be light with your boundary setting and even see it as an experiment or game. You'll probably question your decisions and want to go back and give in. You may ruffle some feathers. If people are used to you behaving in one way, they might need time to adjust to your new way. You might have to repeat yourself and enforce your boundaries—which, yes, is annoying. But those conversations will be short, and your gains will be long: "Hey, Mike, I saw you sent an email at nine last night and I'm just seeing it now. I just wanted you to know that I'm really doing my best to stop checking email after six in the evening, so I wasn't ignoring you. Moving forward, if it's urgent, just text me; otherwise, I'll get back to you as soon as I can the next day." More on how to have those difficult conversations is in Chapter 7 coming up.

When It's Too Hard to Set Boundaries, Borrow Confidence

When I was thirty-seven weeks pregnant, I had the feeling that my OB-GYN wasn't right for me. I tried to ignore the red flags and pretend it would be fine. Finding another doctor in the midst of the pandemic felt daunting. So, each week I asked him questions, trying to assure myself it would be okay. At my thirty-six-week checkup, I asked him about his episiotomy rate, and it turned out to be three times higher than the national average. That freaked me out. I confided in my chiropractor and doula, who validated my concerns. They reminded me that I could change doctors and that it wasn't too late, even at thirty-seven weeks. They gave me permission to listen to myself and reminded me that I didn't owe this doctor anything, not even an explanation. They gave me the confidence to say, "*Fuck this shit*, I deserve better. I deserve to feel at peace when I envision my birth and not worried about whether I'm in good hands." Every woman does.

I changed practices the next day and successfully delivered a baby boy just ten days later. The new practice was exactly what I wanted— they treated me with dignity and involved me in my care decisions versus making decisions for me. Even though my husband and parents had sensed my discomfort with my doctor earlier on and encouraged me to consider other options, somehow it wasn't enough. I needed more support and validation from someone beyond my inner circle. If you don't have confidence yet, just gather more until you do. Who in your life helps you stand your ground? What kind of person could help give it to you?

I encourage clients with a supportive manager to ask them for help around saying no. Ask your manager to be your accountability buddy and to back you up when appropriate. This creates space for you to dialogue about your experience, get reinforcement when you feel wobbly, and receive feedback on your progress. You can even make boundary setting part of your professional development. You can't continue to grow at work if you don't have boundaries. The more senior a leader you become, the more you'll have to say no to say yes to greater responsibility.

If you recognize within yourself that you just don't have the resources to set boundaries, for whatever reason, consider who can help. Take a moment now and make a list of who can support you in embracing your boundaries and staying the course. It can be a friend, a family member, a colleague, a mentor, your boss, a coach, or a therapist. There ain't no shame in doing this with support.

▶ People who could help me set or enforce boundaries are:

_____

_____

Now, the part you've been waiting for. Where do you begin? How do you figure out which boundaries to set and which to prioritize? It can feel overwhelming. Let's start gently, as I did with Jenna. This Boundary Builder exercise provides you with a framework to pinpoint one boundary you can set and practice immediately. Once you notice that the world doesn't stop, that you're safe, and that you actually can benefit from setting a new boundary—you'll get the feedback and courage to keep going for more. Remember, this most likely won't feel natural. Just like when you do strength training, feeling sore means you actually worked your muscle. When you feel awkward, guilty, or uneasy after setting a boundary, you have worked a new set of muscles, too, and are making progress. Don't let the discomfort dissuade you, but allow it to encourage you.

The Boundary Builder

Step 1: Choose a Value or Feeling to Focus On

Because boundaries enable you to be the best version of yourself with more ease, figure out which part of you needs that space to shine. I suggest you look at your values and choose one that you'd like to express more deeply and freely. Hint: You already chose three that you wanted to bolster with your accountability questions—so one of those would be a good place to start. Or choose a feeling that you want to experience more of, such as *vital*, *peaceful*, *creative*, *powerful*, *organized*, or *productive*.

Here's an example:

I'd like to feel more *productive* during the workday. This means I'm able to stay focused and make progress on what matters.

Now it's your turn.

▶ The need, value, or feeling I want to amplify is: _____

_____

Step 2: Name an Activity That Allows You to Experience More of It

What activity would make it easier for you to express this value? Here's an example:

> Maintaining one consistent to-do list (instead of sticky notes, emails, calendar reminders, etc.) will help me feel more productive.

Now it's your turn.

> ► _____ [activity] will help me experience more
>
> _____ [value or feeling you're focusing on].

Step 3: Generate Ideas for Boundaries That Help You Experience the Activity You Identified

To guide you in exploring the possibilities, note the following five prompts. Not all will apply or require a response. You might also have other ideas for boundaries beyond these.

Relationships: What Interactions Do You Need to Start, Stop, Increase, or Decrease?

Our relationships can support us in reaching our desired state or prevent it. What boundaries can you create with people to experience more of the activity you described in Step 2?

Here's an example:

> I want to run my to-do list by my boss in our one-on-one to ensure I'm focusing on the right priorities for the week ahead to be more productive.

Now it's your turn.

► Reflect on how you might shift your interactions with people to experience more of how you want to be:

_____

_____

Time: What Do You Need to Change About Your Schedule?

Consider whether you need to adjust the start time, stop time, or duration of events or meetings. This could also be blocking out time to think, plan, rest, eat, exercise, be with people you care about, or just be with yourself. If you're booked solid, maybe you want to create padding between events to give yourself some slack. I personally like to have empty pockets of time between meetings. I call this *space in between the space*. It helps me transition, be more intentional for the next thing, and grab a snack, rest, or deal with the unexpected.

Many leaders forget to set aside intentional space to reflect on their leadership and plans—to think strategically about their team and the vision they're driving. What boundaries can you create with your time to experience more of what you described in Step 2?

Here's an example:

I'm going to set aside ten minutes at the end of each day to review and update my to-do list to be more productive.

Now it's your turn.

► Reflect on what changes you can make to your schedule to support being more of how you want to be, as described in Step 1:

_____

_____

Beliefs: How Can You Choose a Better Belief?

Research shows that our actions follow our beliefs. Social psychologist Daryl Bem finds that we form conclusions about ourselves by observing our behavior in the same way we form conclusions about others by observing their behavior.[15] Therefore, by acting "as if" we are the person we want to be, we get a chance to renarrate our own story and enact the best-possible outcome. Sure, you might not be perfect, but if you tell yourself that you're the kind of person who gets things done efficiently, your actions will follow! Just pretend you're that person already. Act as if you are and see what happens.

Here's an example of a *limiting belief*:

I'm not an organized person, so it's hard to be productive.

Here's an example of a *supportive belief*:

I'm the kind of person who gets things done efficiently.

Now it's your turn.

▶ Reflect on an unsupportive belief in regard to your desired change. Capture it below.

_____

_____

▶ Now create a supportive belief based on how you'd like to be. Fill in the sentence: "More and more, everyday, I'm the kind of person that is . . ."

_____

_____

Systematizing: What Can You Automate to Reduce How Much You Have to Think and Choose?

Making choices requires mental power. How can you set yourself up for ease? How do you give yourself less opportunity to wiggle out of what you truly want and more energy to go for it? Where do you keep getting stuck, slowed down, or frustrated? If you are consistently dealing with the same roadblocks, how might you design a path around them?

Here's an example:

I consistently feel overwhelmed in the mornings and waste a lot of time just figuring out my plan for the day. I will systematize my planning process. Each evening I will write down my priorities on my to-do list for the following day before I go home. This way, when I arrive at the office, I know exactly what I need to focus on.

Now it's your turn.

▶ Which, if any, systems, processes, or automation techniques might help you experience more of the value or feeling that you described in Step 1?

_____

_____

Environment: How Can You Modify Your Space to Better Support You?

What you see, hear, taste, touch, wear, or interact with makes an imprint on your mood. Notice what brings you down and what elevates you. What can you eliminate, organize, or add to your environment to invite more pleasure, ease, and control in order to express the value or feel the feeling you described in Step 1?

Here's an example:

I'm going to use Evernote to track my to-do's across devices. This way, I'm not looking at ten sticky notes to remind me of what I have to do, and I have access to it on my mobile device.

Now it's your turn.

▶ Reflect on what you can modify in your environment to experience more of the value or feeling you want from Step 1.

_____

_____

Step 4: Choose One

Reflect on the previous boundaries you listed. Which feels the easiest to tackle? Start light. Choose the one that feels most doable. That's the new boundary you're going to set up! Write it down here:

▶ I'm going to implement this boundary:

_____

so that I can _____
[describe the positive outcome or impact of practicing this boundary].

Now consider what obstacle might get in your way. Psychologist Gabriele Oettingen of New York University has dedicated more than twenty years to researching human motivation.[16] She found that it's not enough to focus on our vision; we have to contrast it with our reality to anticipate potential obstacles and create a plan for overcoming them. Oettingen found that focusing on positive outcomes can be so relaxing that it lowers our blood pressure and makes us less likely to take action. When we think about what could go wrong, however, Oettingen found that our blood pressure rises, providing an energizing effect. Consider obstacles when you're feeling grounded and safe. But do avoid catastrophic thinking and spinning out.

➤ When you imagine setting your boundary, notice what resistance shows up, if any. What do you foresee will get in the way?

_____

_____

➤ What do you plan to do when you face your obstacle?

_____

_____

I just want to give you a high five right now. This isn't easy work. If you like the other boundaries you wrote down, pencil in a date to review the list and consider whether you want to tackle more or do the exercise again for other areas. The point is progress—just start with one and take the easiest next step.

Step 5: Notice How It Feels to Implement Your Boundary

After you set up your boundary, give yourself credit for making progress even if it wasn't perfect. Observe whether you feel lighter or uncomfortable as a result. Again, it's normal to feel awkward, guilty, sad, and regretful when you set a new boundary.

Tips for Communicating Your Boundaries

Keep It Short. Setting a boundary with someone only needs to take a minute. Literally. Next time you find yourself dreading the exchange, know it will be over quickly. Your goal is to be clear, concise, and unapologetic (without being aggressive). No need to overexplain. Here are some examples of communicating boundaries.

When You're Invited to a Weekly Meeting That You Don't Need or Want to Attend
"Thanks for including me, but I have to sit this one out because I'm already booked. Amy is representing our team and will plug me in."

When You Want a Colleague to Stop Gossiping About Another Person
"Hey, this conversation isn't feeling right to me. Let's switch to…"

When a Vendor Provides Disappointing Work
"This isn't working for me. I need some time to better respond, so I'd like to get back to you."

When You Don't Want to Answer Emails After Work Hours
"Hi, guys, I really need to honor my family time and can't respond to emails after 8:00 p.m. If there's something extremely urgent, please text me. Otherwise, I'll address it when I log in at 9:00 a.m."

Or consider an email sign-off that says: "I'm responding during my regular work hours, which may not be consistent with yours. Please feel free to respond during a time that works for you."

Does this feel tough to do? No worries, I have you covered. There's an entire chapter on how to master difficult conversations. In Chapter 7, we'll go deeper into developing the courage to ask for what you need and how to say it. But sometimes a simple no is all it takes. If you're an auto-yes kinda person, as in you agree to things without thinking them through or because you feel way too much pressure to please, then drill these words in your mind: "Let me get back to you."

You can add: "Wow, thanks for considering me for this project. I can see it's very important. Let me get back to you by Wednesday once I review my workload. I want to make sure you can get everything you need."

If You Can't Say "No," Delay. Delaying gives you time to consciously make a choice. In that time, you may come up with clarifying questions such as: "Tell me more about what's driving the timing? Does this absolutely have to happen by December 1?" Or "Can you give me some background about this project and why it's important for the team?" Sometimes you may discover things aren't as urgent or important as you may have assumed.

If you're clear you want to say no, a delay gives you time to thoughtfully decline: "Thanks again for considering me. I don't have capacity to take this on at this time. I'm at 100 percent capacity through June, and I don't want to give you crappy work. It's best if you find someone else to do this." You could offer to show them how to do it themselves or recommend someone else. Or, if you think it over and decide to say yes, at least it's a conscious yes versus an automatic one that you may later resent. You can even give a modified yes: "I'll do ABC if you give me support with XYZ."

Stay Gathered. Keep your energy centralized. Imagine your focus as a spotlight that shines from the top of your head through your entire body and comes out of your feet. Keep the light on yourself. It's fine to shine it on others and empathize with their needs. But it can't be at the expense of keeping you in the dark. This isn't about being selfish but is about being responsible. If you're in the dark, resentment and burnout can brew. It's dangerous.

Stay attuned to your experience so you can make more conscious decisions instead of fear-based ones. Pay attention to your body before, during, and after the experience. Remember why this boundary is important to you and let that lead you. If you notice yourself checking out, going numb, freezing, fawning, or becoming confrontational, that's a signal that you need to pause and delay.

Repeat and Reinforce. Deciding to set a boundary is like deciding to get in shape. Clarity and resolve are just the beginning. You don't go to the gym only once; if you'd like to stay in shape, you keep showing up to work out…for the rest of your life! It's a choice you get to keep making, but hopefully it becomes a habit so you don't have to think about it. Boundaries, especially if they don't come naturally to you, require maintenance. It will get easier. New neural pathways will generate. But boundary setting requires vigilance. It's the small wins and consistency over time that will transform your career and life.

Now, are there days, weeks, or even months when you skip the gym? Sure, life happens. But then you start again. So, if you fall into your old ways, just start again the next moment that's available to you. When you fall off track, use your learned optimism voice to regulate: "Oh, there I went, answering emails at midnight. I slipped, but it doesn't mean I'm hopeless [it's not personal]. I know how to get back on track [it's not permanent], and this is just one goal of many that I'm working on [it's not pervasive]." In Chapter 8, we'll discuss how to stay on track.

Lead the Way. Finally, if you can't motivate to set boundaries for your own well-being, do it for others'. (It's a bit twisted…but let's just work with the momentum of a desire to please.) When you set boundaries, you inspire other people to do the same. Sure, some people will be disappointed or upset and have a "how dare you" response (that's their stuff to work through). But you also may be just what's needed to start a ripple effect of well-being and rest and a paradigm shift around self-respect, honoring your body, and being human. I want my children and my team to be empowered to take care of themselves, and it starts with how I show up. Be the change. Now go practice!

Boundaries Practice

Practice delaying your yes if someone asks you for something that you're hesitating on. If you do it, record how it felt during, immediately after, and within the week. If you end up saying no, notice what happens afterward.

▶ Review the boundary you selected to work on and capture it here.

_____

_____

▶ What's the biggest obstacle to making it happen? Create a plan for that.

_____

_____

▶ Write down the smallest action you can take to start. Decide when you'll do it.

_____

_____

CHAPTER 5

Play

How to Deal with Uncertainty

This chapter teaches you the inner skill of holding a playful mindset, the key to managing anxiety in the face of uncertainty. When we confront the unknown, it's easy to worry about what will go wrong. But what if things end up being better than we ever imagined? What if the best-possible scenario is lined up and we just don't know it yet? What if everyone is rooting for us? What if we're actually way more supported than we think? Is it worth feeling crippled by anxiety and sacrificing our present moment, the only moment we really have? Often we suspend living until we resolve uncertainty... "once I earn the promotion, launch the product, finish the book, buy the home, etcetera, then I'll be safe, happy, and relaxed and can breathe." But all that time beforehand matters just as much. That's our life. Using a playful mindset doesn't just keep things feeling lighter but also helps us live better. It doesn't guarantee a happy ending but purifies the air so we can breathe easier along the way.

I had a tri-fuck-ta year in 2019 that was stuffed with uncertainty. My mom was diagnosed with ovarian cancer. I then discovered I was

BRCA1 positive, which means I carry a genetic mutation that puts women at higher risk for ovarian and breast cancer. They recommend removing your ovaries by the age of forty to prevent cancer. I was thirty-eight and had just started in vitro fertilization. No pressure. And then we had two failed IVF procedures.

I felt crushed by dark what-ifs. What if I don't have a second child? What if my mother doesn't make it? What if I get cancer? What if my six-year-old daughter has the *BRCA1* mutation as well? What if the embryo we're trying to use next has it? Do we still use the embryo if it has this genetic mutation? It was a whirlwind. I was afraid to even peek into what life would be like after removing my ovaries. I'd be jumping into surgical menopause. I had heard it could hit you like a train and change your life from the moment you wake up from the anesthesia. The greater the uncertainty, the smaller I felt. I was melting underneath the anxiety. (I guess this was a warm-up for 2020.)

Anxiety is worrying about the future in *anticipation* of a perceived threat. It's a response to what *could* happen, not what's *actually* happening. My worst moments during that time took place in my imagination. Meanwhile, the fleeting yet sane moments took place when I was intentionally activating my playful mindset: I'd stay present, remind myself that I don't know what will happen, and inject a sense of wonder: *What if it works out?* I'd breathe, feel the texture of the couch cushion beneath me, and let my thoughts cling to only what was happening now. I'd ground myself microsecond by microsecond. Staying present felt like I was hopping from one grain of sand to the next. At any moment, if I lost my balance, I'd fall into an abyss of darkness. But so long as I stayed light and focused on the delicate surface of this moment, I was safe. I'll break down how you can activate a playful mindset using the PLAY model in a bit. But, first, let's talk about our relationship with uncertainty.

Our Brain's Job Is to Predict the Future and Eliminate Uncertainty

It doesn't feel natural to be present and to hold space for the unknown. That's because our brain is obsessed with predicting the future. Our brain's number one job is to guess what's next so we can stay alive. This is energetically taxing. It's why too much uncertainty can lead to emotional exhaustion. A little anxiety is not bad, nor is it a disorder. In fact, it can keep us from danger and from making reckless choices. But too much anxiety, the kind that won't go away, can keep us stuck and avoiding opportunities that might be worth exploring. As humans, when facing the unknown we reference our past experiences—that's how our brain makes predictions. Try a quick experiment here to witness your brain at work. Glance at the following text and say aloud what you see:

Th1s b0ok iz gr8t!
1 wsih iy laernd tih$ s00n3r
1tz aLr3@dy h3Lp1ng!

What are *really* in the lines above are black-and-white shapes, a combination of letters, punctuation marks, and numbers. Technically, there is not one real word written there, and yet your brain probably strung together three sentences. You may have read:

This book is great!
I wish I learned this sooner
It's already helping!

Your brain substituted letters for numbers and shapes and even some letters for other letters to stitch together meaning where there was none.

Our brain's main job is to quickly make sense of the ever-changing environment and then orchestrate responses to aid in our survival. We do this automatically so that we know whether to explore further or avoid a situation or person altogether. However, this tendency to jump to assessing, judging, and labeling a situation, person, or collection of letters and numbers may lead us down an incorrect path altogether. For example, a client's boss was acting irritable and yelling constantly. My client was convinced that she'd done something wrong and that it was costing her a promotion. She started to explore working in other departments. It turned out that her boss's wife had been diagnosed with breast cancer, so his behavior had nothing to do with my client. She was relieved and stayed.

What we see is almost always a matter of perspective and not an objective reality. Anil Seth, neuroscientist and author of *Being You: A New Science of Consciousness*, calls this phenomenon *controlled hallucination*.[1] Our unique experience of reality is based on a variety of inputs from our body, our unique past, and even the context of the moment. We think we're experiencing a common reality, but it's more suggestible than it is stable. Because we tend to agree that the sky is blue, ice is cold, and the mountain is tall, reality feels agreed upon. Meanwhile, our mood can transform whether we interpret the question "Can we talk?" as a threat or an ordinary request.

Why Our Brain Tags Uncertainty As a Threat

In some ways, it's easier for our brain to tag uncertainty as a threat. Remember that during any one second we're receiving over eleven million bits of information from our entire body and our brain is paying attention to only forty bits per second. Our attention is like the lens of a video camera. And that camera is capturing the story of our life, or a version of it. Because we have limited perspective, and a negativity bias, if we're not conscious, the camera will zoom in on all the things that are going wrong or that *could* go wrong. Cue the drama.

Uncertainty feels threatening because it's associated with potential loss. When we worry about the future, we're anticipating what to do if we lose something: a promotion, an opportunity, a relationship, or just the way things are. Our brain hates losing more than it loves winning. Nobel laureate Daniel Kahneman and his associate Amos Tversky call this tendency *loss aversion*.[2] Their research reveals that a person will be more upset about losing a hundred-dollar bill than they will be happy about finding a hundred-dollar bill. The amygdala, the fear center of the brain, interprets *any* loss as a loss of resources necessary for survival. This then triggers a stress response. "What if the new boss will hate me and fire me? What if the presentation doesn't go well? What if giving her constructive feedback will ruin our relationship?" Because we spend more energy avoiding loss than focusing on potential gains, we make bad decisions.

This is why I had you start the Work Happiness Method by getting clear on your vision. Focusing on what you want to avoid won't lead you toward what you want to experience. Imagine telling a pilot, "Don't take me to New York City." You could end up in Iceland or Texas. Meanwhile, you were hoping to land at Newark Airport in New Jersey.

Play Embraces the Unknown

The good news is that just as we're wired to worry about the unknown, we're also wired to embrace it. I see our response to the unknown as sitting on a continuum between anxiety and excitement. Consider what it feels like when you try out a new restaurant or plan a vacation to a destination you've never been to. We don't call that feeling uncertainty; we call it novelty.

The difference in how we view the unknown is our mindset. When we're in our playful mindset, we're eager to explore. When we're led by our negativity bias, we're anxious and trying to avoid loss.

What determines whether you approach a situation through the lens of your negativity bias or with a playful mindset is how safe you feel. Polyvagal theory, conceived by Dr. Stephen Porges, posits that our nervous system is constantly patrolling the environment for safety and danger.[3] It's always on and listening, like an Amazon Alexa. Porges calls this *neuroception*. Because neuroception operates on an unconscious level, we could be in fight or flight without even realizing it. When our systems are clenched in a stress response, our experience of the world is also contracted. Instead of seeing the unknown as a chance for positive possibilities, we see it as a threat to defend against. Although we might not be able to prevent the stress response, we can consciously nudge ourselves away from it, toward safety. That's the opportunity for us and the skill we get to build. The goal of mobilizing our playful mindset is to expand our perspective and thereby our possibilities.

If I were to give you a cocktail recipe for a taste of playfulness, it would include these ingredients:

- 3 parts deep presence
- 3 parts curiosity and open-mindedness
- 3 parts optimism
- 1 part risk-taking

- Add the zest of a wink
- Garnish with excitement

Ultimately, playfulness is not about the activity you're engaged with but about your state of being. Ego is out the door. You're not in your head worrying about "how will this make me look?" You're seated deeply in the now, assessing a level of small risk while also feeling safe. Think of a mother playing peekaboo with an infant. When she withdraws and hides, the infant experiences a sense of uncertainty. When the mother reappears wearing a warm facial expression and says, "Boo!" this relieves the infant. Our playful mindset downregulates our autonomic nervous system from a state of high-arousal fight or flight to a place that's more safe and at ease. Play strengthens the efficiency of the neural circuits that can instantaneously downregulate fight-or-flight behaviors. It helps us press the brakes on our stress response.[4] When we're playful, we feel open to possibility, interested, creative, and generally positive. There may be some element of danger, but not enough to hold us back, just enough to draw us in...like it's the start of an adventure.

Play itself is difficult to define. Scholars have written entire books about how difficult it is to define.[5] Play can happen when you're singing in the shower, working on a report, doing the laundry, or even having a disagreement with your significant other. As humans, unlike other animals, we are uniquely designed to be playful through our adult years. That's because playfulness is critical to our well-being.[6]

Play helps us connect. It disarms aggression. You know when someone is playful. You can feel it. You can see it in their body language. When we're playful, our eyes are big and warm, our smile is authentic, and our movements are fluid. You can hear it in someone's tone. You feel welcomed. You make eye contact. Play invites collaboration. It's the foundation for co-regulation, the physiological process of connection. Co-regulation is when two people receive and send signals of safety to one another. They're autonomic defense systems are quieted. Former hostage negotiator and author of *Never Split the Difference: Negotiate As If Your Life Depended on It* Chris Voss describes how play is a critical skill in disarming a threatened individual.[7] The ability to control the inflection of your voice to signal curiosity, deference, and collaboration—basically, playfulness—is the most effective tool for changing a terrorist's mind. If it works on them, it will work on your boss. More on how to master difficult conversations is coming up in Chapter 7.

Playfulness also makes us smarter.[8] It literally sculpts the brain. By helping us navigate an ever-changing world, it encourages neuroplasticity, the creation of new connections between neurons. Neuroscientists Sergio Pellis and Andrew Iwaniuk and biologist John Nelson reported that playfulness predicts brain size in mammals.[9] John Byers, an animal play researcher, discovered that the amount of play an animal experienced is positively correlated with the development of its brain's frontal cortex.[10] That region is responsible for cognition, monitoring thoughts and emotions, language, and more.

TOOL

The PLAY Model

So, how do you feel playful even when you're freaked out about what could happen? How do you make yourself feel more safe when you're worried about the economy, the climate, or what your client will say when you push back on today's deadline? I got you! Let me introduce you to the PLAY model:

- **P**ause and give yourself permission to see the situation differently.
- **L**et go of expectations and how it should go.
- **A**cknowledge your feelings.
- Say **Y**es, and..." to accept the present moment for whatever it is and then to create the next choice for yourself.

Pause and Give Yourself Permission to Be Playful

Take a breath, walk around the block, go into nature, drink some tea, or get a hug. Do anything to signal that you're allowing yourself to shift gears, get quiet, or find comfort. This tells your nervous system that you're safe. To break free from past programming and choose a new way to see, you need to press pause. You need to consciously decide that you're willing to experience a new story. This breaks the auto-stitching of your current reality and allows for more possibilities to swim to the surface. It begins a mindful choosing. All it takes is a microsecond. If you pause, you at least give yourself the chance to make a new choice. It's setting the intention to be agile, curious, hopeful, and optimistic even if done reluctantly. If only 1 percent of you is on board, that's enough to start. This represents you taking control of where you point your camera lens.

How It Sounds

Instead of "I have to," see it as "I get to."

For example, "I have to present our findings" can shift to "I get to share what we learned and influence our next steps."

Take a moment now and try this out on something that feels hard to accomplish. Give it an "I get to" and notice what other thoughts flood in. Notice how your body feels when you do this.

▶ I have to _____ .

▶ I get to _____ .

▶ What am I noticing? _____

Pausing allows you to shift from feeling like something is a heavy obligation to feeling it is an opportunity with lightness. When you pause, you get to ask questions like: "What else can I see? How else can I show up? What is yearning for my attention?"

Let Go of Judgment

Release judging. This one is hard. This is the yang to the ying. What we want to do is control how we see, but to do that, we have to let go.

Let go of what? Consider suspending expectations, assumptions, and judgments of how things should be. Judgment is our brain's attempt to organize and predict based on past experience. Sometimes our assessments are accurate, but sometimes they're not. If you're pushing hard, what would it look like to release the reins?

Letting go can feel scary because it feels like you're giving up your power. But when you let go consciously, you're actually using your power because you're making a choice. It's a paradoxical twist of being in control by letting go of control. During great uncertainty, when you experience anxiety or fear of what the future holds, opt for wonder, curiosity, surprise, and, dare I say, delight (gasp!).

How It Sounds

Instead of dreading a situation and assuming it will suck, get curious. Say to yourself, "I wonder what will happen? How might I be surprised?"

Being curious and willing to be surprised doesn't have to be dramatic. You don't have to lie to yourself that it will be different. You're just opening the window a crack, enough to let in fresh air and a new perspective. Then just see what happens.

Take a moment and script out wonder. Notice what you notice when you do it.

➤ I wonder how _____
[a person, place, thing, or event] will surprise me? Maybe even delight me?

▶ What am I noticing when I inject wonder? _____

_____

Acknowledge the Present Moment and Zoom In

Play only takes place in the present moment. You can't be worried about the future or ruminating about the past. Being present keeps you safe and away from operating in your old programming. It requires being with yourself wherever you are.

Label your emotions, as we discussed in Chapter 1, to help you metabolize them. Notice the sensations in your body, your heart rate, and your breathing and call out what you're experiencing. Practice zooming in on this moment right now. What's the texture of the clothes on your skin right now? What's the temperature of the air? What are the sounds humming in your background? Get into your body.

How It Sounds

Here's an example:

> I'm a bit edgy. I'm scared that I'll mess this up in front of everyone. My body is clenched. I'm a bit sweaty. The sun is shining. The air conditioner is humming. Those red flowers are pretty. Jeez, I just don't feel like going into that room.

Try labeling your emotions now.

▶ What's true in this moment is that I feel _____ .

I'm seeing _____ , I'm hearing _____ ,

I'm touching _____ .

▶ This is what I am noticing: _____

_____

Say "Yes, and . . .": Accept Reality and Then Create the Next Moment

This step is inspired by the art of improvisation, a form of live theater in which the plot, characters, and dialogue are made up in the moment. A seminal rule of improvisation is to build on whatever your teammate just said by starting your part with "Yes, and..." This requires accepting and agreeing to the reality that's been set up—the *yes*—and then gives you a turn to create what's next—the *and*. For example, if a teammate says, "An alien landed in a radio station." The following person builds on that by saying: "*Yes, and* that alien wanted to hear Beyoncé's latest song." This step embodies how we dance with what we can't control and with what we can. It's surrendering to the present reality and then choosing your response to it.

How It Sounds

Here's an example:

> Yes, I'm scared that I'll mess this up in front of everyone. And I'm going to give it my best anyway even if my voice is shaky. I know I have a lot to offer.

> Your turn to try it:

▶ *Yes*, I accept that the reality is _____ , *and* what I

can choose next is to _____ .

▶ This is what I am noticing: _____

_____

How Julia Used the Playful Mindset

My client Julia joined an exciting start-up as the director of design. Six months into her gig, she still felt like an outsider and had no idea whether she belonged at this company. She was steeped in uncertainty. The cool kids wouldn't invite her to the important meetings. When she proposed ideas, she felt like they were ignored. Even when it came to big design conversations, the product manager, Kevin, would run the show. It was making her extremely anxious and keeping her up at night. She couldn't make an impact no matter how hard she pushed. She'd never been treated this way at work. She didn't know what was going on. Was it her? Was it them? Was it something else?

She joined my coaching program because she was questioning herself. Everything she tried didn't work. She saw no way forward, but she didn't want to give up.

On our first coaching call, Julia stated that she had three goals:

1. To develop a trusting relationship with the product manager, Kevin
2. To stand up for herself and feel heard
3. To establish the design process at her organization and make a positive impact

That week, Kevin scheduled a meeting to discuss the project Julia had been working on for months. This was a big deal. The only problem was that Kevin sent the meeting invite only one day in advance and Julia would be traveling during the proposed meeting time. Meanwhile, eight people accepted the invitation almost immediately. Julia couldn't help but feel cornered. But she needed to be in that meeting. She was panicking. To help her navigate this tricky situation, I nudged her to use her playful mindset. Here's how she applied the steps.

Pause: Julia Gave Herself Permission to See Things Differently

Before we spoke, she was already visualizing how she'd take the call in the middle of the airport. Everyone else was going to be there in person. Once again, she felt like she was going to be on the outside.

I encouraged Julia to pause and consider other possibilities. What if they rescheduled? How might this be an opportunity? Julia was scared to ask Kevin to move the meeting and to inconvenience nine people. But at the same time she realized it was a step toward one of her goals, to stand up for herself.

Instead of moving into a state of obligation, "I have to take this meeting virtually and be accommodating," Julia was able to pause and reframe: "I get to practice standing up for myself to Kevin. That's an important goal of mine. I guess this could be a chance to build a trusting relationship, too. If I ask to reschedule and it doesn't happen, at least I did everything I could. If it does get rescheduled, I get to influence the project and make the best-possible contribution."

Let Go of Judgment: Julia Released the Idea That Kevin Hated Her

I asked Julia if she could momentarily let go of the idea that Kevin disliked her. It could be true, but it could also be wrong. What if there's something else going on that she's just not aware of? Is that possible? What if Kevin respects her work and needs her help, but he's been slammed on his deadlines and didn't realize she felt left out? What if he's never worked with a design director and doesn't really know how to collaborate with her or where to let her in?

Julia really liked this. She instantly felt a change in her body and noticed herself relaxing: "Well, actually, it's true that this group has never had a design leader and I don't think they know what they're supposed to do. Maybe if I approach him with curiosity and try to understand what's driving the meeting and the timing, I can learn something about where he's coming from. I can help him understand how I can contribute."

Acknowledge: Julia Labeled Her Feelings and What Was Coming Up in the Present Moment

Julia told me she was nervous and worried. But she was also starting to feel excited and more free. She was going in eyes wide open.

Say "Yes, and...": Julia Accepted the Dynamics with This Team and Stepped Toward Influencing Them Where She Could

Yes, this wasn't what she signed up for when she took the job. Yes, this was the most challenging social dynamic she'd ever faced personally and professionally. Yes, Kevin made it difficult for her to participate in a meeting that was very important. Yes, she hasn't felt part of the team since she began. Yes, her asking to reschedule would be asking nine people to change their plans.

And...she had a lot to contribute and wanted the best for the team. And...she wanted to collaborate. And...she wanted to be of service and understand what was driving this timing. And...she chose to reach out to Kevin immediately after our conversation.

The Result

Julia said it was the best conversation she's had with Kevin since she started. She was able to learn why Kevin rushed the meeting. She was able to help him understand the importance of her presence. He rescheduled it and took her advice about how to structure the meeting.

Although she continued to be uncertain about her future at this organization, she started to wonder with a bit more hope and a little less anxiety. She realized it wasn't personal. She also learned something about how to approach difficult conversations (more on that in Chapter 7).

How I Used a Playful Mindset in My Situation

As I shared earlier, when I was thirty-eight I learned that I'd need to remove my ovaries by the age of forty to help prevent ovarian cancer.

I was dealing with the crisis of my mom's cancer, my unsuccessful IVF procedures, and the dread of surgery.

Thank God that my mom did great and is thriving. She is a tremendous woman who embodies courage and positivity. After giving up on having a second child, I got pregnant naturally in the midst of the pandemic at the age of thirty-nine. My boy, Lev, gave us all so much hope in such a hard time.

I'm not promising happy endings but am offering you a way to make the journey with more grace. I wove in and out of the playful mindset constantly to help me face uncertainty. Following are a number of examples. Mine is not as tidy as Julia's story because it wasn't one specific event but rather a complex series of circumstances over many years.

Pause: How I Gave Myself Permission to See Things Differently

I remember thinking, "I don't know how to do *this*. I don't know how to deal with my mom's illness and how to support her. I don't know how to deal with my own condition and how to support myself. I don't know how to deal with a pandemic." It was all sorts of uncertainty.

I just kept reaching for more perspectives when I felt stuck. It's not about ignoring what sucks or diminishing it. It's about being willing to see more.

- Instead of "I have to drive my mom to the doctor," I saw it as "I get to spend quality time with my mom."
- Instead of "I have to get my ovaries removed and go into menopause," I saw it as "I get to be proactive about my health and set myself up for minimal risk."
- Instead of "I have to accept we won't get pregnant," I saw it as "We get to embrace the ease that comes with having an older kid. Europe here we come!"
- Instead of "I have to labor with a mask on," I saw it as "I get to have my husband in the room."

Let Go of Judgment: How I Released Expectations, Judgment, and Assumptions

When it came to my oophorectomies and hysterectomy, I let go of the dread of surgery and started to wonder how I might be surprised by this experience, maybe even delighted. Letting go of the dread took me about eighteen months. I'm capturing this as a point in a sentence, but I want to underscore that there's no timeline. Letting go sounds effortless, but conscious unraveling requires strength in other places so you can surrender in just the right spot. It may require support from others. My spiritual mentor helped me focus on the phrase "graceful transition." I was able to relax into a place of faith. What is letting go and feeling safe but faith that it will somehow work out? It was either let go or just be doomed.

To help me, I began to wonder how this might actually be part of some grand design. I imagined life without PMS and periods and saw glimmers of optimism. To shift my anxiety, I steadied myself with information. I spoke to several other women in similar circumstances. I was intentional about who I spoke with and what questions I asked. I did a "Discovery Tour"—more on that in the next chapter. I learned about hormone therapy and went from fearing it to embracing it as the option that would help me.

Acknowledge: I Labeled My Emotions and Clung to the Present Moment

Again, this is a cross-sectional slice of a multilevel experience. I started working with a therapist to help me acknowledge and process. The closer I got to my surgery, the more I rested on the shore of it, letting the waves of whatever came up wash over me. I was angry, scared, overwhelmed, resentful, but mostly sad.

How would I care for a baby, recover from pregnancy, get surgery, recover from that, get menopause, and still do everything else? In my head, I'd start to feel sad for my body; sad for my baby, who I wouldn't be able to pick up for six weeks; sad for my seven-year-old girl, who'd get whatever energetic scraps I had left; and sad for my husband, who'd be picking up the pieces. I was pissed that this was putting stress on so many and delaying important projects and business. It sucked.

Say "Yes, and…": I Accepted the Situation As Is While Creating the Best-Possible Setup

Yes, I have the *BRCA1* mutation and its risks. Yes, I'm going to have surgery and get menopause immediately. And…I'm going to get as much support as I can with childcare. My sister-in-law offered to stay with us for three weeks to help me recover and care for the kids. And…I'm going to use any resources I have to support my healing and integration of this experience. And…I'm going to self-care by blocking my schedule for six weeks. And…I'm going to take those hormones to support my well-being.

Using your playful mindset doesn't have to be tidy or even sequential. Slow down and just go for what's available to you. Play with your playful mindset!

Play Practice

▶ Reflect on whether an uncertain outcome is filling you with anxiety, fear, worry, or dread. Write that down here:

I'm worried about _____

because this could happen: _____ .

▶ **Pause** and give yourself a chance to reframe.

Is there a heavy feeling of obligation that you might be able to substitute with the feelings of opportunity and possibility?

(continues)

(continued)

Instead of "I have to _____

_____."

What's your "I get to"?

"I get to _____

_____."

▶ **Let go** of judgment and expectations.

How might you inject curiosity into a place where you feel convinced it just won't go your way?

"I wonder _____

_____."

▶ **Acknowledge** your feelings.

"I feel _____

_____."

▶ Say **"Yes, and..."**

"Yes, this is the reality: _____

_____."

"And...here's what I can choose next: _____

_____."

CHAPTER 6

Discovery

How to Explore New Roles and Responsibilities

If you're not happy or in love with your current role, don't quit just yet. In fact, you might have everything you need right in front of you. Quitting too soon might deny you the opportunity to grow deeply, and it can cost you. It takes a ton of time and energy to interview. It takes even more to establish yourself at a new organization—you have to build new relationships, prove yourself, and get up to speed. When my clients are on the verge of resigning, I often tell them that this is an exciting opportunity for them to use their job as a laboratory for their professional (or personal) development. Remember, if you're willing to quit, then you have the option to be brave.

On the flip side, if you're content with your current experience but are wondering about what's next or what else you should be striving for, this chapter will serve you in sorting out the uncertainty.

To figure out what changes you need to make, if any, or how to make your career even more fulfilling, this chapter offers practical steps to help you navigate ambiguity. At this point, you've developed your vision, are practicing your values, and have set new boundaries. You learned how to tune in to your playful mindset in the face of uncertainty. Now let's talk about how to be efficient in exploring what's next. How can you amplify what you want to experience and dial down what's draining? Whenever you're feeling unclear, unsure, or stuck, all you have to do is gather information. This chapter teaches you how to discover it.

Job Crafting Is Customizing Your Role for More Fulfillment

Psychologists Amy Wrzesniewski, Jane E. Dutton, and Justin Berg call the process of designing your dream role *job crafting*.[1] It's when employees customize their role so they can experience more meaning and satisfaction. It's a bottom-up approach as opposed to traditional job design, where managers define responsibilities and expectations from the top down. We can job craft in three areas:

1. *Task crafting* is when we identify which responsibilities we want to add or let go. How can we spend more of our day doing what energizes us? For example, a manager may decide to delegate routine meetings to other staffers to allow herself to focus on higher-value strategic projects instead. Take stock— what tasks do you want to do more of and which do you want to release?

2. *Relational crafting* is determining which relationships we want to strengthen or modify. How can we change the nature or the extent of our interactions? For example, a salesperson may decide to spend more time in person with his clients to foster deeper connection. Take stock—what relationships or interactions do you want to dial up or down to feel more energized at work?

3. *Cognitive crafting* is reframing how we see our work. It's transforming a job into a calling. It's going from just earning a paycheck to contributing to something bigger. How can we better connect the dots between what we do and who we serve? For example, a school bus driver sees herself as a community member. She helps kids get a good education by transporting them to school safely. Hint: By answering your accountability questions, you're naturally weaving together how your work helps you be who you want to be.

Which of your buckets needs adjustment? It can be more than one. Remember, your end goal is realizing your vision. So, what shifts will help you get closer to being the kind of person you want to be?

If you filled out the Energy Inventory Tracker in Chapter 4, it might illuminate some areas you want to play with. Or take stock now. Track what you do for several days. Then, identify each task and interaction as energizing, draining, in scope, or out of scope. That way, you can quickly scan and identify which, if any, adjustments to make. A client I work with realized he wasn't involved in enough strategic work, so he made space in his calendar to just think. Another client noticed they were underutilizing their direct report and gave the person more responsibility. See if you can identify one small, one medium, and one big adjustment that would help you feel more fulfilled. If none of the choices you see in front of you are appealing, if they're too intimidating, or if you're still unclear, keep reading!

To help you refine what specifically to do, use the following series of strategies to gather the information you need. Depending on your energy level, schedule, and responsibilities, you may not be able or want to use all these strategies. Gauge what feels right and skip over the rest. There are times in our lives when we're not ready for change.

Doing nothing is also a choice. If that's the case, consider the very first strategy below, relaxation.

Relax

Don't push. Do nothing. Take a nap. Sometimes actively thinking about our problem doesn't help us come up with creative solutions. In our brain, the default mode network is a group of regions that fire up when we're *not* actively focused, and those same regions lay low when we are.[2] Daydreaming, for example, is when the default mode network gets busy below the surface, making connections.

When we're charting a new path, we can't always walk in a straight line. Intentionally weave in time to relax and unwind to support yourself in integrating all the information you're gathering without conscious effort. I know it feels counterproductive. But it's important to trust forces beyond your control that support your transformation. Just as daffodils seemingly appear out of nowhere, even breaking through a snowy surface, the clarity you're aching for may spring up if you give yourself a season to chill or even just ten minutes to lay down.

When we're feeling full, we need to listen and take a break. Do laundry, walk the dog, take a hot shower, or chitchat with a friend. You can also tell yourself, "I'm going to give myself two months before I actively start to do anything else." Create a boundary around relaxing and see what emerges.

Brainstorm Possibilities in Stages

When you're ready to ideate, be conscious of your brainstorming process. Gathering information and being open to possibilities require divergent thinking, which feels like a big inhale. After you get full of information and ideas, it's time for convergent thinking: the process of analyzing and narrowing down those possibilities—taking a big exhale. To explore a solution to a complex challenge—whether it's innovating the next big tech gadget or knowing what to do with our career—we often engage in an alternating series of divergent and con-vergent thinking. It looks like this.[3]

Noise / Uncertainty / Patterns / Insights   Clarity / Focus

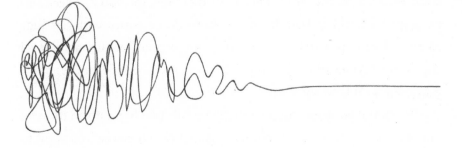

Research & Synthesis   Concept / Prototype   Design

With each round, the choices are narrowed until you feel confident that you're looking in the right direction. Often, I see people get stuck when they try to conduct divergent and convergent thinking at the same time. Just as you can't inhale and exhale at the same time, you won't get far in your exploration if you instantly cut off ideas as they arrive. That's why I encourage my clients to take time to fully explore their ideas and gather information so they can formulate the proper stance on what to do.

For example, a working mother of two young kids, Anna, found herself at a crossroads, unsure of what was next. She signed up for executive coaching because she was working until ten o'clock each night, feeling frustrated with her team and tormented by guilt for not spending more time with her kids. As a rising star, she had unique expertise in a fast-growing field. She didn't know what to do and how to best take advantage of her position while also balancing her family life and well-being. If she joined another organization, would it be any better? Would she see her kids even less? She was swirling and stuck.

When I encouraged her to describe her ideal day, she started by describing how she would have time to pick up her kids from school and make space for organizing Girl Scouts meetings with her daughter. She then stopped abruptly—it was like the needle of a record player screeching across the vinyl. This was ridiculous, she noted. There was no way she could fathom having time to do activities with her kids as even a near possibility, so what was the point of this activity? I encouraged Anna to keep going. This was just a brief exercise, and I promised we'd land somewhere realistic.

If you find yourself stopping in the middle of a brainstorm to weed out or criticize ideas, you're bound to get stuck. Of course you want to analyze what's feasible, but not until after you inhale big and acknowledge what's possible. Are you record screeching? Fast-forward three months after that meeting. Anna indeed founded a Girl Scouts troop, was picking up her kids from school each day, and, in fact, had so much extra time each day she started to explore how else to fill it.

Let's practice divergent thinking for three minutes. Set a timer. Go ahead and list as many ideas as you have on how to improve your sense of fulfillment at work right now. Look at your vision and values for inspiration. Go for quantity over quality, and don't edit your ideas or do any record-screeching halts. Avoid judging them as good, bad, realistic, and so forth.

▶ **Divergent Round 1:** All the Ways I Can Improve My Job or Career (3 Minutes)

_____

_____

_____

_____

_____

_____

_____

_____

_____

_____

▶ **Convergent Round 1:** Circle the ideas that feel worth exploring further right now. Give yourself one minute.

▶ **Divergent Round 2:** Take the ideas you circled and see whether you can expand on them or come up with even more ideas based on the direction they point. Give yourself two minutes.

_____

_____

_____

_____

_____

_____

_____

_____

_____

► **Convergent Round 2:** Circle one to three ideas and decide how you might explore them further. Consider using some of the following strategies.

Talk to Your Boss

Sometimes talking to your boss can be the most efficient route to discovering what's possible. In a healthy organization, a manager's success relies not only on their employees' performance but also on their employees' level of engagement and development. Sometimes bosses just happen to be clueless about what their employees need to flourish. They can't read your mind. Complain all you want about it, or just have a two-minute conversation. A quick talk with your boss can save you a tremendous amount of inner turmoil and discovery work. First, identify what type of information you're missing.

I can't tell you how many people I've coached who regretted waiting so long to talk to their boss. In the next chapter, we'll walk through the important steps of how to prepare yourself for this conversation, but the basics can literally take you less than sixty seconds to say.

Here are the sentences you can use to elicit information from your boss:

► *Set the intention that this is about being of service:* I want to do an excellent job and contribute even more deeply...

► *Describe the missing information:* In order to do that, it would be helpful to understand...

► *Affirm how your boss is helping you be a better performer:* I'm confident once I have this [info/feedback/guidance/opportunity], I'll be making an even greater impact...

The key is to get clear on what information you're missing and are asking for. It usually falls into one of four buckets: feedback, guidance, role clarity and expectations, and missing perspective. Let's dive into each scenario.

Talk to Your Boss About Missing Feedback

You may be getting one-sided feedback. For example, your boss may be very clear on what has to improve but rarely acknowledges what you're doing well. That can leave you feeling insecure and wondering whether you're in the right place. This was the case for my client Maria, a civil engineer who was suffering from imposter syndrome. She felt so insecure that she started to explore other careers. I encouraged her to have a conversation with the principals of her firm to gather information about her performance and to validate her—whether indeed she was great at her job or she needed more guidance. They had no clue Maria had been starved for feedback. Because she was doing such a great job, they assumed she didn't need anything from them. The next day, she found a gift card to her favorite lunch spot on her desk, and moving forward they set up a weekly meeting for Maria to get full feedback and validation on her decisions. It was a game changer. She confidently stepped into her leadership role and learned to trust her instincts.

If all you hear is praise and suspect there's something more, you can ask for that information as well. For example, my client Sachin had been denied a promotion twice, but he continued to excel in all his goals. He was growing frustrated and felt like management was hiding something. He acknowledged that information was missing and asked for specific examples of how else he could grow. His boss agreed that he was exceeding his performance goals but that he was failing to build strategic relationships with leadership within the global organization. It turns out Sachin just wasn't liked. It seemed like all he cared about were goals and not the people who worked for him. This was really tough to hear. But it gave Sachin the focus he needed to improve. He began to schedule virtual coffees, ask different questions, give more praise to his team, show more care, and over six months not only was he up for his new promotion, but he also felt like a more noble leader.

What you want is *full feedback*. Encourage your boss to let you know where else you can improve or to acknowledge where you're excelling. It's not needy; it's responsible. It's you being proactive. It shows you care about your work. It's human to want to grow and be seen. If you don't get that type of reinforcement, your work will suffer. Feedback is a key criterion to experiencing flow, the ultimate performance state, which is important to keeping you engaged in the immediate term.[4] Feedback is also a critical criterion for developing grit, which is about staying engaged in the long term, despite the obstacles.[5]

Utilize these statements to elicit feedback:

- ▶ I want to do an excellent job and contribute even more deeply.

- ▶ In order to do that, it would be helpful to understand where [I'm excelling so I can continue to amplify that] and/or [where I have room to grow and improve].

- ▶ I'm confident once I have this type of feedback, I'll be making an even greater impact because I'll know I'm on the right track.

- ▶ You don't have to tell me on the spot, but perhaps in our next one-on-one, could you specify where [I am meeting or exceeding expectations and/or where I can do better]?

Talk to Your Boss About Missing Guidance

Perhaps you're working independently and need mentorship on how to handle a situation, a relationship, or a project. If you're spinning your wheels trying to find a way forward, it may be time to raise your hand and ask for help. Often, we think we have to have all the answers; meanwhile, that type of thinking just wastes a lot of time. Of course you want to show that you've done all you could to problem solve, but there's a fine line between resourcefulness and foolishness. Asking for help is not a sign of weakness; not asking for help at the right moment is.

If your drive to do it all on your own is getting in the way—that earnestness in being proactive may turn into obstinance. You risk wasting not only your own time but also that of your team. Now that more people work remotely, it's difficult to casually ask for help. But do it anyway. If you don't know what you need help on but sense you could be doing something better, that's also a great thing to ask: "I'd love your advice. I don't know what I don't know. How might I approach this challenge better? If you were in my shoes, what advice would you be seeking?"

Utilize these statements to elicit guidance:

- I want to do an excellent job and contribute even more deeply.

- In order to do that, it would be helpful to understand [how to connect with the clients better/how to get accounting to respond faster/how to pull the sales numbers, etc.].

- Here's what I tried: [a, b, c], and here's what I learned: [x, y, z].

- I'm reaching out for help because I don't want to compromise the timing of this project.

- I'm confident once I have this guidance, I'll be making an even greater impact.

Talk to Your Boss About Role Clarity and Expectations

If you're finding yourself doing too much, it may be because you're experiencing *role creep*. That's when you take on more than what's within your scope of responsibility. It can happen because your team isn't staffed appropriately, you're an overachiever, the role isn't clearly defined, or management is giving you mixed signals on what they want. You need to get clear on what's expected and where your role starts and ends. It may be that your role needs to be rechartered. That's not a bad thing. In fact, that's an opening for you to job craft. If you're the one who has been taking on more, ask your boss for support in saying no. This way, your boss has your back and you're not penalized. Borrow support from them to stay in your lane. Reference Chapter 4 on boundaries if you need a refresher.

My client Tasha worked as an HR business partner and was always being asked to join committees and participate in meetings that were outside her role. She loved helping, but it was too much. She felt confused about what to do and she hesitated saying no. I encouraged her to ask her boss to clarify whether she should participate in certain activities. Her boss acknowledged that she shouldn't. Tasha's boss spoke to other leaders, acting as reinforcement for Tasha, and Tasha consulted her boss case by case. Because they made this exercise explicit, they created space to discuss it openly at her one-on-ones. Tasha now feels more sturdy and confident about what she needs to do and what she doesn't.

Utilize these statements for setting expectations and gaining role clarity:

> ▶ I want to do an excellent job and contribute even more deeply.

> ▶ In order to do that, it would be helpful to understand the scope of my role more clearly.

- Here's what I've been doing: [provide specific list], and here's what I believe was the original scope of my role: [provide job description or other documentation].

- I'm reaching out to get clarity because it's important for me to meet your expectations and I'd like your support in finding a way to keep to those boundaries. [If you want to change something about your role, mention it.]

- I'm confident once we can agree on my role, I'll be making an even greater impact.

Talk to Your Boss About Missing Perspective on Growth Opportunities

What seems difficult for you to see or figure out may take your boss a one-minute phone call. You don't have the big-picture view of all the possibilities, roles, openings, or projects in formation. Talking to your boss can be the most efficient way to job craft. Pursuing growth opportunities doesn't always mean going after a promotion or more money. Growth opportunities ideally are means for you to make a greater impact on the organization in a way that levels up your strengths, aligns with your values, and steers you toward your vision. Sometimes all you need to do is communicate to your boss the conditions that would help you flourish and ask them if they know of a way to customize your experience to help you do that more. Your boss can help you tweak your responsibilities, assign you to exciting projects, or connect you with key stakeholders to make your job more energizing. Let your boss help you ideate what's possible.

For example, my client Maya thrives when she gets to solve big, complex problems. Meanwhile, her team's budget was cut and they were forced to stand by and maintain what they had built. She was growing restless and depressed. She couldn't see a way out. She needed a big challenge to sink her teeth into. She spoke to her boss about her values around strategic problem-solving and how energizing it was for her to turn chaotic messes into streamlined processes. He immediately got her a meeting with the CEO, and she participated in several organizational culture transformations. Her role didn't technically change, but she got the exciting project she was aching for.

It's not always about craving more work but sometimes about downshifting. My client Alexander hated being a manager and yearned to be an independent contributor again. As an engineer, Alexander loved coding and dreaded his managerial tasks. Feeling ashamed that he didn't enjoy this natural career progression, Alexander assumed he'd need to find a job at another company. I coached him on how to bring this up with his manager. His manager returned Alexander to his individual contributor status with relative ease and speed. Instead of directly managing employees, Alexander could mentor folks informally. Meanwhile, Alexander could take on more complex engineering projects and spend his time doing what he loved again.

Utilize these statements for discussing growth opportunities:

- I want to do an excellent job and contribute even more deeply.

- In order to do that, it would be helpful to understand how I can continue to grow.

- I'm reaching out to explore what's possible and get your advice on how to grow—whether it's trying out a new project, responsibility, role, collaboration, or something else. I'm open to possibilities that would enable me to [do x, y, or z] or [leverage my values of a, b, and c] or [move me closer to my ultimate dream of e, f, and g]. I don't have a specific idea in mind and was hoping we could brainstorm together or that you might have purview over opportunities I'm not aware of.

▶ I'm confident that when I have a chance to [do more x, y, or z] or [be more a, b, and c] or [get closer to e, f, and g], I'll be making an even greater impact.

I can't promise or predict how things will go for you when you talk to your boss. But by gathering more information, you'll reduce the uncertainty and be better equipped to make the next right decision. Even if the conversation doesn't immediately land you in a more fulfilling place, you'll have more information on what will. If you're hoping for a change and your boss doesn't give you a glimmer of hope that things can be different, that in itself is very valuable information and quite telling.

Label Change As an Experiment

Let's say you identified an adjustment you want to make. Perhaps it's working from home twice a week or doing your one-on-ones in a new way. Whatever the change, label it an experiment. This tends to relax you and others involved because it doesn't feel like a permanent change. Labeling something an experiment makes it easier for your boss to agree, if you need permission. It also gives you a chance to try something new and learn. It provides you and those involved with the flexibility to adjust as you go along. Of course, you'll have to decide what's next after the experimental period, but by then you'll feel more certain about your options, and so will others. (Need help asking for this? That's coming up in Chapter 7.)

Labeling any small change an experiment invites trial and error, encourages communication, and feels more collaborative. My client Sierra wasn't comfortable letting go of running the weekly status meeting. When we called it an experiment, that gave Sierra a sense of control because she knew she could always return to the way things were before if it didn't work out. When you label something an experiment, create a clear deadline and agree on how you'll assess moving forward so everyone is on the same page and feels safe.

Immerse Yourself to Explore

This is a twist on calling it an experiment, more a try-before-you-buy technique. If you're eyeing a new project, role, team, or career but don't know enough about it—shadow others, go to a conference, ask to participate in key meetings, or be a fly on the wall. This is above and beyond your normal duties, but as long as you can do both and your boss doesn't feel like it will affect your work, you have a good chance of learning.

When I was an account coordinator in advertising, I knew I wanted to be a strategic planner. The company wasn't accepting people without experience or graduate degrees into that role. I asked to shadow the head of the department and help out with whatever she gave me. It took me about a year to get that opportunity to shadow. Another year later, I made the transition to full-time strategic planner. I was the youngest person they had accepted into that department. That boss is still my mentor to this day.

Lead the Learning

When you lead the learning, you create the means for others and yourself to learn and explore. You can host a podcast, organize a lunch and learn, or write a newsletter. This type of effort requires extra work, obviously. Depending on how many experiences you produce, it can become another job, so start small with just one thing to see if you like it.

Personally, I love this method because it's a triple win: You win by learning. Others win by learning. The organization wins by fostering learning. Plus, as the host of such events, you position yourself as a leader. I've used this strategy continually to propel my leadership. It started in college when I created a club to learn about marketing professions. We invited influential industry experts to speak. This gave me a chance to network, and I ended up scoring an internship from that experience. It also helped hundreds of other students find and pursue opportunities as well.

Go on a Discovery Tour (aka an Informational Interview)

A Discovery Tour is when you talk to people about what it's like to do what they do, be in their shoes, and work with others. I encourage my clients to see themselves as tourists learning about new places and cultures. This makes the discovery process feel more fun and takes the edge off. Use that sense of tourism as you gather information about possible ways you can deepen your fulfillment at work. There's no pressure to figure it out or commit because you're doing this purely for the love of exploration. You control the pace—maybe it's a conversation once a week or once a month.

I encourage clients to describe this tour as part of a "discovery period" so it takes the pressure off of decision-making. This makes the person you're interviewing feel at ease because they often can't control hiring or don't want to mislead you about an opportunity. A Discovery Tour is more than just "picking someone's brain." It's a thoughtful inquiry. What do you want to see or get to know during your visit? Just like travel, it depends on your particular interests and values. I help my clients create a conversation itinerary.

How to Conduct a Discovery Tour to Figure Out What's Next

Every friend, family member, colleague, boss, former colleague, professional organization member, and social media contact can help you get the info you need to feel confident about your next move.

Your neighbor's cousin could know the person you need to speak to. If you're squirming with discomfort and making excuses why conducting an informational interview isn't for you, I understand. I've heard: "But, Stella, I'm not connected." "But, Stella, I'm not on social media." "But, Stella, I don't like networking." "But, Stella, I can't admit I don't know what I want." "But, Stella, I don't have time to do this." I hear you. All of those things can be true *and* you'll still be able to make this happen and actually be grateful you did.

Let's discuss your biggest hurdle to a Discovery Tour. Vulnerability. Often, my clients procrastinate on reaching out because they feel vulnerable admitting that they don't know something or that they're asking for help. But every client who has tried a Discovery Tour is relieved after their first one. When you admit that you're trying to figure out what will help you feel more alive and that you're opening yourself up to learn, other people will feel two things: (1) inspired by you—I can't tell you how often clients report back that the folks they interviewed expressed wanting to do something similar; and (2) honored. By asking for advice and help, you're being deferential. It's signaling that you respect someone enough to seek their support. This gives them a boost. It helps them feel like they get to contribute to something bigger than themselves. Telling you their story helps them create meaning in their narrative. If you're worried that you're creating more work for others, I encourage you to reframe it as "I'm giving them a chance to give back, reflect, and get heart centered." It's nutritive for the both of you if you let it be. Just as you want to feel fulfilled and have a sense of meaning—so do others. Just as you want your efforts to ladder up to something that matters—so do they. Helping another human get a little clearer on their path is an easy way to get a hit of that.

Each conversation is a chance to learn. It may not be conclusive, but it will be illuminating. That's a win. Don't feel disappointed if after one exchange you don't have everything figured out. My hope for you is that you have more questions and that you've narrowed your set of possibilities just a bit. Learning that you don't like something is as important as realizing that you do. I recommend my clients have at least five to ten conversations before they make any decisions. It does take time to do this due diligence. But it also takes a lot of time to step into a new role, be trained, realize you hate it, and then try to figure out something else on the side. So do the work up front even if it's uncomfortable.

Let's discuss how to get these informational interviews done using the least amount of energy. There's no time to waste.

Get Organized with a Resource Tracker

First, set up a Resource Tracker that lists everyone you know or want to contact. Remember, even your neighbor's mom can be a resource. You never know who someone knows. I like to use Excel to stay organized. You can find my template at workhappinessmethod.com/download or scan the QR code with your smartphone.

The Resource Tracker helps you keep track of the folks you're reaching out to. It also serves as a visual display of how supported you are. When you gaze at your list of names, know that you're held by a community. Even if you haven't spoken to someone in twenty years, know they want to help. Go ahead and even list entire communities, such as your alumni group, employee resource groups, Facebook groups. If you're feeling shaky, you're not alone. Most people do. Just know at this stage all you're doing is organizing. As you'll see in the following small example, I like to rate my comfort level with each person on a scale of 1 to 5, where 1 is *Not Much* and 5 is *Very Much*. You can also indicate VIPs. This helps you sort your list so you can easily start

Comfort 1 = Not Much 5 = Very Much	Name	Email Address	Phone Number	Social Media	Notes	Status
5	Biana Grishan	biana.grishan@gmail.com	(734) 668-8418	@bianagrishan IG	She mentioned her friend, who is an editor.	Waiting
5	Mike Lowry	mike.lowry@blinds.com	(818) 543-9687	NA	His wife works in PR and offered to help.	Connected
3	Maplemeadows Moms FB Group	NA	NA	@MaplemeadowsMoms	Ask if anyone works in film.	Planning
VIP	Jenn Soo	jenn.soo@companyxyz.com	(432) 678-8910	@jennsoo2	Wait until she returns from honeymoon in August.	Planning

with the people you feel safe with. Depending on how deep you want to go, you can even color-code rows to indicate the status of reaching out:

Green = We've Connected
Yellow = Reached Out and Waiting to Hear Back
Red = They Can't Help at This Time

Reach Out in Batches

Second, do outreach in batches. Start with ten people you feel most comfortable with. I encourage my clients to go for quantity. If there's a handful of VIPs, sure, contact them individually. But if you write a heartfelt note (see the following template), it's totally fine to send it to ten, twenty, or fifty people at a time. Gulp. I know that can feel like a lot. But I encourage you to blast multiple contacts at once. Here's why:

- *You're busy.* You'll see, customizing an email for each of twenty people takes a lot of time. It will become a barrier to getting the information you need. Communicating in batches also helps more people know what you're looking for.
- *People are busy.* They're away on vacation, dealing with a sick loved one, or in the midst of a launch. If you want to connect, it may take them several weeks to respond and then another several weeks to meet. It's unlikely that your schedule will immediately get out of hand.

Sample Email Message to Book Discovery Tours

Here's a sample email message:

Hi there,

This is a bit uncomfortable to write, but I'm hoping you can help.

[Be honest. If it doesn't feel uncomfortable, don't write that. But opening with vulnerability is real, not weak. People respond to it because it's honest and brave.]

I've spent the last five years in [Role] at [Company] and I love it and the people. I'm proud of achieving [a, b, and c].

[Do a quick statement of where you are now, your position, and an exciting achievement. Don't be bashful. Let them know you're amazing.]

But I'm getting the sense that there's something bigger for me to do—but I don't know what it is. Here's where you come in.

[Describe what's driving your outreach. Is it growth, better leveraging of your strengths, figuring out your passion, finding a side project?]

I'm giving myself the next three months to just talk and explore what's out there. Perhaps I need to advance my leadership skills, focus on a new product, or start taking flute lessons. Who knows?

[If you're uncomfortable with ambiguity, labeling and time-boxing this phase make it feel more controlled. That also takes the pressure off this being a job hunt.]

Will you scan the following and connect me with anyone who might have experience in these areas? I'm not looking for a new job or to make any big moves. I just want to explore what's out there, hear people's stories, and get a glimpse into roles and worlds beyond mine. This way, I can consciously direct my career.

- Cutting-edge technology in agriculture, sustainability, and education (I know, it's a wide range)
- Collaborating with system thinkers
- Anyone who works at the cross section of design, product management, and data
- Successful company cultures where people are first
- Service leadership
- Anyone who works at companies [x, y, or z]

[I like to use bold font and bullet points where possible. People scan emails and don't read. So this makes it easier for them to identify key information. The more specific the better.]

If it's helpful for connecting purposes, here's my LinkedIn.

[You can also provide a blurb. Don't stress about making your LinkedIn perfect. Just make it good enough.]

Also, if you know of any conferences or resources I should look into, I'm open.

Thanks so much for your willingness to help. I'll keep you posted.

Best,
[Your Name]

Now you're ready to have an actual conversation with someone. Below is your conversation itinerary with all the stops you want to make during your Discovery Tour. It's a suggested flow for talking to someone and gathering information. I've arranged the talking points in bullet points to make it easier to digest. You probably won't have time to ask everything. Choose what feels right and prioritize based on your needs. It's also okay if you prepare a list of points you want to cover and it goes off script. Just like traveling is an adventure, these informational interviews can be, too!

Conversation Itinerary

A Script for Your Informational Interview

Start with Gratitude and a Quick Briefing

- Thanks so much for meeting with me. It really means a lot.

- I want to honor your time—so I just want to make sure you're good until _____ .

- To give you some context, I'm exploring [how to grow/how to leverage my skills in new ways/more about the company/my next move] and I just want to learn as much as I can.

- I'm giving myself the next _____ [weeks/months] to take it all in (I'm calling it my Discovery Phase) before I even start analyzing or trying to do anything with my learning.

- I have a background in _____ and my current job is serving as _____ .

- Before that, I did _____ .

- What I value is _____ , and I thrive when _____ .

- I'm here because [I really admire your _____ /I'm curious about what you do/I want to learn more about a company like yours/I want to learn about your industry/ Tom told me you're passionate about what you do—and I just want to hear your story].

Get Their Story

- Can we start with you? Tell me your story. How did you end up choosing this [role/industry/company]?

- Wow, I really admire how you _____ . (If appropriate, acknowledge the strength, courage, or beauty in their story.)

- What's a typical day like for you?

- What's most energizing about what you do? What's a bit draining?

- What do you wish you knew before you [started this project/took this job/joined this department/entered this career]?

Dive into Specifics

- What skills are essential to excel in this [project/job/ department/industry/career]?

- How might I develop these skills?

- How is success defined and typically measured?

- How have you seen people from different backgrounds join?

- Where do you see this [project/job/department/industry/ career] going in five years?

- What are the vibe and culture like?

- Do you have formally identified values? If so, how do you see them practiced? What do you appreciate about the [process/team/leadership] here?

- What do you wish was different about the [process/team/ leadership] here?

(continues)

(continued)

Values Match

Design specific questions based on your specific values. Don't be afraid to ask about the things that matter. Here are a few examples:

If your value is Innovation you can ask:

- Describe the creative process. How does an idea become reality here?
- Which leaders, teams, or organizations embody this level of innovation?
- How much do you invest in research?

If your value is Work–Life Balance you can ask:

- How common is it for people to work from home?
- How does this [role/team/organization/field] support people with small children?
- What hours are people expected to work?

If your value is Collaboration you could ask:

- Tell me about the balance between how much one works independently versus with others?
- How supported do you feel by your teammates and leader?
- How do people handle conflict?

Ask for Advice (That They Can Give)

- What advice do you have for me if I want to learn more about _____ or get a role doing _____?
- How would you position my shifting into this new [responsibility/project/job/field]?
- What questions would you ask if you were in my position?
- Based on your knowledge, what kind of role would complement my values around _____ and desire to _____?

Ask for a Connection or Resource

- I'm trying to learn as much as I can in this Discovery Phase. Would you mind connecting me with additional folks? I'd be respectful of their time and we could even do a phone or Zoom call. And, of course, it would be strictly informational (no job-seeking pressure).

- Do you know someone who does [x, y, or z—be as specific as possible]? Do you know someone who has gone through [a, b, or c]? Do you know someone who works [in/at] _____ [include departments/fields/ organizations]?

- What resources should I check out? Classes, events, industry organizations, websites, etc.

Appreciate and Share What You Learned

- Thanks so much for your time today.

- I'm feeling even more [clear/excited/energized/ knowledgeable].

- I really appreciate that I got the chance to hear your story and how you _____ .

- Your insights regarding [a, b, and c] were really powerful.

- You saved me a lot of time and research.

- I'm going to [check out that website/conference or give your friend a call] and then I'll keep in touch with an occasional email if that's okay with you.

I recommend taking notes either during or after your conversation. Mark up questions, energizing signals, and red flags. Notice how your body feels during the exchange.

Keep Them Posted

Send an email thank-you note right away or a handwritten note. A small gift is also always appreciated, especially if you want to deepen your relationship. It can be a thoughtful gift

(continues)

(continued)

(you heard Tom mention he loves cupcakes, so you have them delivered). Or it can be a gift card to a coffee shop. Definitely follow up after you meet with their contact to thank them.

Discovery Practice

Let's review all the ways you go from ambiguity to clarity. You'll start by considering ways to customize your role, aka job crafting, to feel more fulfilled. There are three buckets you can play in:

- *Task crafting* is when you identify which responsibilities you want to add or let go.
- *Relational crafting* is determining which relationships you want to strengthen or modify.
- *Cognitive crafting* is reframing how you see your work, transforming a job into a calling.

Seven Ways to Explore Job Crafting

1. Do nothing, relax, and let your default mode network connect the dots for you.
2. Brainstorm in stages, alternating between divergent and convergent thinking.
3. Talk to your boss about giving you information, whether it's feedback, support, role clarity, or growth opportunities.
4. Try a small change and call it an experiment to give yourself flexibility to explore without a commitment.
5. Immerse yourself in a new possibility to get a feel for the experience.

6. Lead the learning by hosting events, recording a podcast, or writing a newsletter.

7. Take a Discovery Tour and conduct informational interviews.

▶ Are you ready to discover ways to be more fulfilled at work? Which aforementioned strategy resonates with you?

_____

_____

▶ Consider a plan to explore. What's the smallest first step you can take?

▶ When will you take that first step?

_____

CHAPTER 7

Approach

How to Transform Confrontations into Conversations

This chapter will support you if you don't know where to begin or what to say in a difficult conversation. If you're stuck in passive-aggressive madness or dealing with a bully, this information will help transform your dynamic. If you're struggling to advocate for yourself, whether asking for more pay, appreciation, or a new assignment, I got you covered. If you're crying in the bathroom because your boss is a micromanager and you're worried he can't take your constructive criticism, this is for you. If you want to deliver negative feedback that supports versus insults, this is the key. The techniques I share in this chapter help you establish illuminating and deep connection. They apply to the office and beyond—even to deal with that neighbor who complains about your dog. The process can be as gratifying as the outcome. Even if you have already asked and failed, this will teach you how to come back effectively. The opportunity here, if mastered, is that you will not only get what you need but also get more. You get to grow.

Why Your Energy Is Everything

Most people fail before they even begin to talk, and that's because most people start with the wrong approach. There are two ways you can broach a difficult topic: as a conversation, signaling trust, or as a confrontation, signaling threat. Your approach represents your energy, and your energy is *everything*. Readying your approach is probably the most difficult part of a difficult conversation. Shaping your approach is the focus of this chapter. Numerous wonderful resources exist on how to be persuasive, negotiate, and deliver feedback. But what often is overlooked is the approach. I'm placing the magnifying glass on this invisible inner work, the fulcrum on which connection and safety hinge.

Readying their approach is often the work people skip, dismiss, or don't even know exists. Not being intentional about your approach is like painting a room without taping off the molding, covering the floor, and removing the furniture. It can become a sloppy mess—a mess that you have to clean up, retouch, or redo completely. The prep work takes time, can feel annoyingly tedious, and can even be complicated. But, if done well, the paint job itself is more effective. The same goes for your difficult encounter. If you prep your approach well and stick with it, you'll experience more grace. But, hey, if you have to repaint, it's not the end of the world! We'll talk about that, too. It's never too late.

Your approach determines everything because emotions, just like viruses, are contagious. That means you're transmitting your inner experience during an encounter. If you're feeling resentful, angry, judgmental, or disappointed, the other person will feel it on some level. Your message begins from within yourself. We're wired to connect, read one another, and call bullshit if the words do not match the energy. I'm not asking you to stop feeling your feelings—but when you speak, you don't want to be possessed by them.

I'm sure that you've had someone apologize to you with their words, but not mean it...and that felt icky and unsatisfying because it wasn't authentic. But you've also had someone say sorry in a way that melted your heart and evoked instant forgiveness. We've evolved to read each other's energy—so we can decipher whether a person is safe to be around or not. Your approach signals the state of your nervous system in that moment. Your facial cues, vocal tone, and body language speak louder than your words.[1]

That's because, as mammals, we are designed to co-regulate with each other. This means our brains and our bodies attune to one another's, often within microseconds, unconsciously. Mirror neurons facilitate this co-regulation—we mirror another's expressions and then get information about the other's state. Not only do we mirror facial expressions and body movements, but we can also mirror another's brain activity. This is called *brain coupling*. Researchers observed this phenomenon when they did an experiment with individuals using a functional MRI (fMRI) machine, which measures and maps brain activity.[2] One group told a real-life story. The other group listened to a recording of the story. Researchers then compared the brain activity of the speaker with that of the listener and observed that the listener's brain activity mirrored the speaker's with a bit of time lag. On occasion, the listener's brain even predicted what the speaker's brain would do next.

When we communicate, we can literally join the same wavelength as others, especially if our approach is in conversation mode. Even the cadence of breath, menstrual cycles, and walking steps can synchronize when we're together and on the same page.[3]

Confrontation Mode Signals Threat

Let's dig into the difference between a conversational and a confrontational approach. When our approach is confrontational, our body is in fight-or-flight mode. The flight part exhibits itself as avoidance, which is how most people deal with difficult topics. The fight part means that we're readying ourselves for battle, to play offense or defense. Stress hormones are released. Cortisol is pumping through the veins. Just thinking about the confrontation can make us sweat. The heart rate increases. We tense up.

Confrontation mode means we're battling to be right, struggling for power. We're out to prove why we deserve the raise, why Amy's feedback was inappropriate, why we should push back on the deadline. In confrontation mode, our mindset is rigid and convinced: "They better promote me or I'm out of here." "Eva has a problem and is ruining our team." Or "He'll never budge on the timeline." When our approach is confrontational, the situation feels black and white, right or wrong. Options seem limited. There will be a winner and a loser. There's less listening and more talking. We're focused on remembering the argument we prepared rather than staying in the moment, listening and learning. This makes it difficult to reflect, which is why people become reactive and things escalate. A confrontational approach doesn't usually end well. Even if you win, you still risk losing connection and trust.

Conversation Mode Signals Safety

Meanwhile, when we approach the situation as a conversation, the intention is to gather information and reveal what's really going on. To do so, we utilize our playful mindset, which gives our approach a sense of openness, curiosity, and wonder. "Maybe John will surprise us. Maybe there's something we don't know about this situation yet. I wonder what we'll learn?" It doesn't mean we have to agree with someone else's perspective, or they, ours. It just means we're both willing to listen and get to know where the other is coming from. People feel heard and seen. Things slow down. There are silent breaks. There's space to process. There are pockets for possibilities to emerge.

Approaching any dynamic with a willingness to understand, and even to learn, is transformational. One plus one becomes three. You two together amount to something more magnificent than you would be on your own. Perhaps it's not just about option A or B, but maybe an option C, D, or Z might emerge. Instead of it feeling like two sides pitted against each other, there's a sense of togetherness. Conversations, approached well, are fueled by oxytocin. Oxytocin, aka the bonding hormone, is most commonly associated with mothers and babies.[4] It's released during childbirth and breastfeeding. But it's also linked to moments of warm connection such as hugging a friend or petting a dog. Oxytocin lowers stress and anxiety.[5] It helps regulate our emotional responses and cultivate feelings of trust, empathy, positive memories, and positive communication. Basically, you want to be an oxytocin-emitting being. That way, you're signaling safety and loving-kindness, a desire to care and extend compassion.

Here's a quick glance at the differences between confrontation mode and conversation mode.

	Confrontation Mode	Conversation Mode
Objective	To battle, defend, or command	To share understanding
Outlook	Convinced	Curious
Emotional state	Pessimistic	Optimistic
Body	Unsafe: Stress hormones	Safe: Oxytocin release
Relationship	Me versus them	Us
Tempo	Escalating	De-escalating
Options	Limited: A or B	Emerging possibilities
Outcome	Winner and loser or loser and loser	Transformation

A Conversational Approach Gets Better Results

Our approach is a choice. And sometimes it's the only thing we get to control. It's our greatest lever for influence, connection, and ultimately growth. If you don't get your approach right, you risk miscommunication. Intentionally orienting yourself into a conversational approach will dramatically affect the outcome of your interaction more than anything else you do. Not only will you get better results, but it also feels so much better. It's more casual, human, dare I say, fun. Doesn't the intention to have a conversation versus a confrontation just feel lighter? I don't know about you, but my shoulders relax a smidge whenever I frame things in this way. It goes from heavy to light.

My client Caroline had been promoted to lead a high-profile project, but pretty soon after starting, she realized that her manager made no space for her to have autonomy and make decisions. Instead of running meetings, she felt unnecessary, small, and micromanaged. Caroline was mad that she couldn't lead and contribute at a level she was capable of. She was convinced there was nothing that could be done and that she'd tried everything. She avoided talking to her boss for months because she felt like it would be a big confrontation. She was convinced he wouldn't understand and would get upset, and that would only make things worse. She believed her only option was to find another job. She began to interview, but her presence was off. She couldn't show up empowered because she was feeling defeated during the day. It was affecting everything.

Often, managers are unaware of the impact they're having on employees. But it's typically not in their interest for employees to suffer. I urged Caroline to have a conversation with her boss. If she was already interviewing, what did she have to lose? It took her several months to ready her approach. We'll talk about how to do that in a bit.

She finally found her moment. Instead of being mad and convinced there was no way out, she let herself become vulnerable, open, and even empathetic with her manager. She was willing to see things from his perspective. When they spoke, she compassionately acknowledged that her being on the project was probably complicating things for him as well. He confided that he, too, was struggling with how to make it work. They connected. They discussed the undiscussables. *Undiscussables* is a term coined by organization theorist Chris Argyris to describe the topics that feel too awkward, threatening, or embarrassing to address.[6] In a matter of fifteen minutes, it occurred to Caroline's manager that he could find a new project for Caroline. (Side note: This is why I urge you to talk to your boss during your discovery phase—see Chapter 6.) Had Caroline not approached him in this open, conversational way, she may have remained stuck and depressed for a while longer. After this talk, she stopped crying at work. She created a team that she was proud of.

Not only did that conversation give her a resolution to her present work issue, but it was also transformative in her development. That's what excites me most about this work. It taught her to be willing to be playful, to go into the unknown and explore possibilities that she didn't know existed. It taught Caroline that she didn't always have to have the answers or solutions. And, frankly, you can't. She realized that she didn't have to be so alone in her struggle. You can't always see what's available, but you can make your needs known. Often, leaders have greater purview, and though you may not know of a project that meets your needs—they might. When you approach difficult topics as just a conversation and not a confrontation, you gain perspective and new options may emerge.

Now it's your turn. Let's run through how you can go into a difficult conversation. I will walk you through how to embody the conversational approach and then guide you in what to say once you're actually talking.

How to Prepare and Maintain Your Conversational Approach: The Three Ss

Readying yourself for a conversation versus a confrontation has three parts, the Three Ss:

1. Shift your energy
2. Sort your story
3. Stay in empathy

Ideally, this preparation is something you can work on before you talk, but remember to also maintain this approach during the dialogue.

Shifting Your Energy

Shifting your energy refers to doing whatever you can to downregulate your nervous system from stress to safety so you're emitting a sense of openness and curiosity. The best thing you can do is give yourself some time.

Though the actual conversation may be only a few minutes long, the energetic preparation may take longer—hours, days, weeks, or beyond. That's why, ideally, you wait until you've shifted. Don't hit reply to that triggering text, Slack message, or email. Create any kind of space you can. The opportunity to transform and grow begins with *this* type of intentional beginning. You're already winning by engaging in this conscious process of self-awareness and self-regulation.

I'm often asked, "But what if I'm caught off guard and someone confronts me?" Do your best to pause and either delay or reset. Here's what that could sound like:

- *Delay:* "Look, I'm not my best and I want to give you my best. Can we press pause and resume this once I have a moment to [reflect/breathe/rest/eat/think this through/process what happened]?"

- *Reset together:* "Okay, I wasn't expecting to have this conversation in this moment. I do want to give you my full attention and listen deeply, but my mind is all over the place. Can we both take a moment to reset? Let's set the intention to do this with openness, fairness, and kindness. If we start to lose it—let's take a break and resume when we're more grounded. Does that sound okay?"

- *Reset alone:* Sometimes you can't get away, you can't pause, and there's no room to reset together. Perhaps there's a child or adult throwing a tantrum. Or you're in the middle of a meeting that has to keep going. I like to imagine turning a dial up to the number 10, which represents optimal conversation mode. I quickly notice where I'm at. I take a breath and visualize myself turning the knob just one notch closer to 10. I keep at this little by little. I take long exhales. I notice the sensations in my body as feedback. I silently label my emotions to acknowledge where I'm at. See if you can soften and set the intention to learn something new.

Consider using any of the tools we previously covered to help you further manage your mood and shift your energy:

Self-compassion
Learned optimism
Complaint Vacation
Gratitude
Exercise
Spending time in nature
Connecting with friends
Deep breathing with long exhales
Eating well and stabilizing your blood sugar
Rest
Playful mindset

Sorting Your Story

The most difficult conversation you have to have is with yourself first. Sorting your story before you speak forces you to slow down and get clear. This reduces the chances that you'll show up reactive, judgmental, defensive, or offensive. It detangles what actually happened from potential triggers that connect you to past experiences—which may have nothing to do with this event. Sorting your story beforehand helps you organize your thoughts, feelings, needs, and desires so you're clear on your experience and message.

There are five steps to sorting your story, the Five Fs: frame, facts, feeling, foundation, and future. You can use these five steps as a baseline script for your conversation. What I love about this process is that it changes your perspective and elevates the ask. It is inspired by Marshall Rosenberg's Nonviolent Communication framework, which uses nonviolence to help people meet one another's needs in a compassionate way.[7]

> ## The Five Fs
>
> TOOL
>
> Sort your story with the Five Fs—slow down to get clear on what happened and what you're hoping for:
>
> **Frame:** What's the win-win intention that's attractive and true for you both?
>
> **Facts:** What specifically happened that upset you?
>
> **Feeling:** How did you feel and what was the consequence of your feeling that way?
>
> **Foundation:** What value, condition, or desire was compromised that's essential for your comfort, well-being, or optimal performance?
>
> **Future:** What specific actions would support your foundation and fit into the frame?

Frame: What's the Win-Win Intention?

By framing your conversation with a win-win intention up front, you create the conditions for this to be collaborative and creative. A win-win framing is one that benefits you both through growth, improvement, or learning. As an opener, it makes the topic feel not only safe but also attractive to discuss. See the following example:

> "David, I want to talk about how we can be successful as a team and support each other in being our best."

Facts: What Specifically Happened That Upset You?

State only the indisputable facts. *When, where, who,* and *what*. When you start with just the facts, it focuses attention on what happened versus what you're worried could happen.

Avoid addressing *why* at this stage. Generalizing, judging, or giving your opinion about the other person's behavior can muddy your perception and send you down the wrong path. For example, saying to yourself "David just doesn't care about this team" or "David is always disorganized" is not necessarily true and can amplify your negative feelings unnecessarily.

Furthermore, when you speak to the other person, if you go beyond the facts, it will shut them down and close the door to communication. They'll get defensive.

Because starting a difficult conversation with someone isn't easy, it's okay to acknowledge discomfort or vulnerability. If anything, that level of honesty is disarming. See the following example:

> "This isn't the easiest conversation for me to have, but I value us being on the same page. This is about when you came in twenty minutes late last Thursday and Friday."

Feeling: How Did You Feel and What Was the Consequence of Your Feeling That Way?

Describe the emotional impact of the facts you observed. Label the specific emotion. This helps you metabolize the feeling and moves your focus into your prefrontal cortex, the planning part of your brain, and away from the amygdala, the fear center of the brain. Avoid blame. Start with "I felt" and not "You made me feel." If another person were in your shoes, they might have different feelings. There are no wrong feelings to have. Just notice what you notice. You can reference the emotion list at workhappinessmethod .com/download or scan the QR code with your smartphone to help you specify the sensation coming up for you.

Most people don't share their emotions because it either feels too vulnerable or inappropriate. Or they assume their feelings are obvious. Emotions are personalized data points that help us understand the impact of events. To establish a desire for the other party to understand, you have to give them data points to work with. We expect people to see what we see, hear what we hear, and feel what we feel. By just explaining the facts, don't assume they'll arrive at your same conclusion or understand your experience. Remember, we're each experiencing millions and millions of data points in our body per second. The other person's nervous system might just be picking up on a different reality. You have to *spell* it out. Explain how you're feeling and what that's stirring for you. This way, the other person can connect the dots. See the following example:

> "I want to share what was happening for me 'behind the scenes' so you can understand the impact it had on me. I covered for you by running the status meeting. I felt really anxious when I led the status meeting unexpectedly."

Foundation: What Value, Condition, or Desire Was Compromised That's Essential for Your Comfort, Well-Being, or Optimal Performance?

Naming what part of your foundation got compromised connects the dots and explains the source of your feeling. By sorting your story to yourself first, you get to recognize the foundational need that was disturbed by the event. Getting to the foundation is digging a bit deeper. There's no right or wrong foundation—it's just a description of what's important for you to be your best. By articulating this to yourself first, it helps you develop self-compassion. When you share your foundation, it helps the other person understand why what happened really matters. See the following example, where "predictability in my schedule" is the foundation:

> "I do my best work when I know what to expect. It's really important for me to have predictability in my schedule."

Future: What Specific Actions Would Support Your Foundation and Fit into the Frame?

The specific actions that you propose should be very detailed, actionable, and clear. Because the future relies on the both of you, choosing the future requires collaboration. Therefore, this statement is an invitation, not a command. It should tie back to the win-win intention you set at the beginning and support your foundation. Describe a *who*, *what*, *when*, *where*, and *how*, but avoid statements that describe how you want someone to *be*, such as "be more professional, proactive, and organized," unless you follow up with specific instructions on what those terms mean. Otherwise, the conversation might wander into fuzzy territory. For example, "be on time" for Juan means arriving ten minutes early. For David, arriving five minutes late is actually on time.

When you sort your story and consider your future, visualize what behaviors, actions, words, or choices would make a satisfying difference. Know that once you speak with the other person, you might cocreate an even better future. See the following example:

> "If you know that you can't make it at two o'clock, could you text me by one that day to give me a chance to get the status report ready? This way, I can best represent our team and won't feel as stressed. Would that work for you?"

Staying in Empathy

The third part of maintaining a conversational approach is to stay empathetic. This refers to consistently being willing to walk in the other person's shoes and see things from their perspective. You stay generous in your assessment of their reactions without blaming them or receiving blame. You demonstrate care and don't take things personally. Even if you disagree with them. It can be really hard to do this. Keep breathing. Here are three ways you can bolster empathy.

Loving-Kindness Meditation

One of my favorite ways of developing empathy and staying there, especially when there's friction with another, is to practice a loving-kindness meditation (LKM). LKM, also known as *Metta*, is a Buddhist practice of wishing yourself and other people well. It's also an evidence-based technique to generate empathy. Researchers at Stanford University found that after practicing just seven minutes of loving-kindness meditation, people reported feelings of greater social connection, even to strangers.[8] Neuroscientific meditation researcher Richard Davidson at the University of Wisconsin found that LKM changes the brain by activating the insula, the part responsible for our ability to empathize with others and make ourselves aware of emotional and physical present-moment experiences.[9] It activates the temporal parietal juncture (TPJ), which also processes empathy and altruistic behavior. Other studies found that LKM reduces the stress response in the body (goodbye, confrontation mode) and reduces inflammation. LKM has been found to increase positive emotions and ultimately life satisfaction.[10] Yes, give me all of that! Here's how you do it.

Loving-Kindness Meditation

TOOL

Bring up an image of yourself and repeat this mantra to yourself:

May you be healthy.

May you be happy.

May you be peaceful.

May you be safe.

Then bring up an image of a person you care for deeply and send them the blessings. See them expressing their heartfelt thanks. Then imagine another person or group of people and send them the blessings. Once you're warmed up and feel softening in your heart, turn to the person with whom you need to speak. Send them the blessings.

My clients often say, "You want me to do what?! To wish that asshole peace, safety, and good health?" Yes, yes I do. You want miraculous results? It starts with you. Can you find space in your heart to wish this other person well in their life? It may take you time and practice to authentically experience loving-kindness in regard to this person. Doing a loving-kindness meditation is not only helpful for your upcoming difficult conversation but also healing for your heart. If you want bonus points, visualize everyone giving you the blessings, including the person you need to speak with!

See Them As a Child

If I'm too caught up in my emotions and feel a brick wall between myself and another person, it helps me to imagine them as a child. I evoke aspects of their personality that are innocent and good. This helps me develop compassion and catalyzes curiosity.

Anything that draws you into another's shoes and enhances your empathy will support you in a difficult conversation. You can do this as a stand-alone practice or do the LKM envisioning the child version of the person you need to connect with.

See Them As a Child

TOOL

Visualize the person with whom you're dealing in their childhood. Get curious. Open your heart. Ask yourself:

How did they end up like this? Maybe they weren't loved or listened to? Maybe they had to fight to be heard? Maybe they experienced a lot of loss? Such a level of inquiry can open you up to consider that maybe they're going through a tough time now and none of this is about you.

Mirror Their Words

Just as we unconsciously mirror one another's expressions to connect with each other, we can intentionally mirror another's words to demonstrate we're listening. Chris Voss, negotiation expert, uses this technique to bond with an individual, make them feel safe, and get them to open up.[11] All you have to do is repeat the last three words (or the critical one to three words) of what someone just said.

Late employee: "Oh, I'm sorry I've haven't been on time to the status meeting. I've just been so tired."

Manager: "Been so tired?"

Late employee: "Yes, my baby is going through a sleep regression and I've been waking up two to three times per night. I'm just not myself recently. I'm sorry about that."

The manager may have assumed that the lateness was a sign of disengagement. Now they understand it has to do with a baby crying. This helps the manager develop authentic empathy.

Try mirroring. It's a graceful way to encourage someone to open up and share more. Then you can get the real story and connect better. That's what we want in conversation, shared understanding, which helps us arrive at better solutions.

Mirror Their Words

TOOL

To demonstrate empathy, repeat the last three words or key words of what someone said. Do this with inflection to signal a question or curiosity. This shows that you're listening and desiring to understand more. It encourages them to expand on what they just said. This opens the doors to deeper understanding.

Listen and Label Their Five Fs

Once you're in conversation, constantly listen for what the other person's experience may be. Are they looking through the same frame? What facts, feelings, foundations, and future might they speak of? Label it out loud. Even if you're completely off—you'll demonstrate and embody empathy. It shows that you care enough to try to understand. It signals that you're making space for their point of view. That keeps the lines of communication open and encourages them to either share more or correct what you're guessing.

> **Manager:** "I know you care about this project [Frame]. Your baby has been keeping you up at night [Fact]. It sounds like you're exhausted [Feeling]. Perhaps you could use some flexibility [Foundation]? Would you like me to take care of the status meetings for the rest of this month [Future]? This way, you get some extra bandwidth, and I'm fine with it as long as I know what to expect."
>
> **Late employee:** "Oh, wow. I was afraid to ask for that. But that would be amazing. I really appreciate that!"

The manager, who previously was feeling anxious, now has more perspective and understanding. Both parties are having their needs met. The manager doesn't experience last-minute surprises and the employee is given some flexibility. Notice how the solution is different from the request the manager made, yet it actually supports the win-win intention of being successful as a team and supporting one another. When you listen and discover what each other's needs are, you can often create a better solution than you even imagined. That's the beauty of a conversational versus a confrontational approach.

Listen and Label Their Five Fs

TOOL

Listen for the other person's Five Fs. Say them aloud to emit empathy. This cues that you're trying to understand—even if you're off. Just deliver it in a way that's curious with inflection, so it leaves an opening for them to expand on what you're observing.

A Few Other Tips to Ready Your Approach

Here are a few more ideas you can use to prepare yourself for a fruitful difficult conversation.

Always Try to Meet in Person, in a Videoconference, or at Least by Phone

Prioritize meeting in person. Don't have a conversation over email, Slack, Messenger, or any medium that uses just text. Seeing someone's face, mouth, and body language and hearing their tone help our brain comprehend.[12] If you're leaving important communication up to an email, the message will most likely be perceived based on the recipient's mood. If they are feeling threatened or uneasy, for any reason—reasons that have nothing to do with you—then your neutral or even positive message will be deemed anything but. Things get lost in translation in text-based messages. Just pick up the phone, hop on a video call, or swing by their office so your conversational approach comes through.

Invite Them to Talk When It's a Good Time

Alright, you're feeling good with your approach and you're ready. But it doesn't mean that they are. This is so basic, but please don't just barge into their office, nab them at the water cooler, or squeeze a conversation in at the end of your one-on-one. Instead, ask the other person when would be a good time. You don't want to be rushed or cut off. Plus, with time pressure, they may not be able to relax enough to hear you. Just as you need the space to ready yourself, so do they. Put yourself in their shoes. If they've had intense back-to-back meetings, they might not be optimized for optimism.

What if there's never a good time? Okay, but if you schedule in advance, at least they won't be caught off guard. Do the best with what you have.

If a Conversation Doesn't Go Well, Repair It

We all mess up and say things we regret. Or we leave things unsaid. Or we contemplate the situation and change our minds. You can always repair. Repairing in difficult conversations doesn't just return things to where they were—it can often make them better. When you repair, not only do you grow, but you offer healing to yourself (and possibly the other person). It's not easy but it is brave. When you're heart-centered and speak your truth, miracles can occur. Deeper connections can forge. To repair, redo your 3Ss to shift your energy, sort your story, and stay in empathy. Plus consider the following openers.

Repair a Conversation

If you regret how you behaved, acknowledge your mistake and how it made someone feel.

Simply say: "I'm sorry that I _____. It must have made you feel _____."

It's healing to take responsibility for your actions. Sometimes we avoid acknowledging our role by saying, "I'm sorry that you feel this way." That only makes the other person feel unseen.

If you froze or forgot to say something important.

Say: "Thank you for speaking last Friday. I realized that I failed to mention something very important to me. When would be a good time to share it with you?"

If you changed your mind.

Say: "I've had a chance to think through what we discussed and have some additional insights. When would be a good time?"

Approach Practice

Take a moment now to practice sorting your story for an upcoming difficult conversation. If you don't have one coming up, consider doing it for a past conversation. Notice what you notice.

Frame

▶ What's an authentic win-win intention that makes this topic feel safe and attractive to discuss for everyone? What's the ultimate goal?

_____

_____

_____

_____

_____

Facts

▶ What specifically happened that upset you?

_____

_____

_____

_____

_____

Feeling

▶ How did you feel and what was the consequence?

_____

_____

_____

_____

Foundation

▶ What value, condition, or desire was compromised that's essential for your comfort, well-being, or optimal performance?

_____

_____

_____

_____

Future

▶ What specific actions can the other person take to address your need?

_____

_____

_____

_____

CHAPTER 8

Refocus

How to Return to What Matters (Without Pushing So Hard)

To refocus means to return to yourself and what matters when you inevitably hit a setback, get derailed, feel stuck, or are lost. The great aikido master Morihei Ueshiba said, "It's not that I don't get off-center. I correct so fast that no one can see." The work in the Work Happiness Method is not to stay glued to your path no matter what. The work is to listen to yourself and what's needed in the moment. Refocusing is guiding yourself back to center as gracefully as possible when you get triggered into a state that's defensive, offensive, hopeless, or unloving. In fact, the process of refocusing acknowledges that there is value in getting "offtrack."

Refocusing is a willingness to see an obstacle not only for what it blocks but also for what it opens. We can reference our own history for evidence of how very difficult moments can give way to transformative outcomes. For example, in my story of suffering through several bouts of Nutella comas, burnout, and imposter syndrome, I found my way here, to writing this book and to a career I love helping others. Researchers call this process of growth through challenging circumstances *post-traumatic growth*.[1] Take a moment now and recount a challenge, loss, or failure that set you up for greater opportunities, deeper connection, and more meaning at work and in your life. Notice whether it took some time for the transformation to take place. It sure did for me. Even when you can't fathom how a dark experience may lend itself to something brighter, refocusing is trusting in what you can't see *yet*.

Refocusing isn't necessarily about returning to your goals but about returning to what's true. Several great books have been written on how to stay focused, maximize your willpower, enhance your grit, and set smarter goals. Those are all important abilities. But we can't always be in a push-forward position, forcing ourselves to achieve more. We must also know how to yield to life and allow ourselves to get pulled back into alignment with our best self, the version we describe in our vision. Especially in America, as in many industrialized nations, we live in a grind culture that prioritizes productivity over humanity, that is, it's toxic productivity. We're already more than equipped and inclined to push through. I want to offer a balancing perspective to help you hear the part of you that rests in love for yourself and others. It's the you that's in harmony with contributing in a way that's sustainable and generative.

When we find ourselves in a place we'd rather not be—whether it's constant friction with a colleague, procrastinating on a report, stuck looking at a blank page, failing to deliver results, overwhelmed with impossible deadlines, eating a fourth piece of cake, waking up in the middle of the night with a sick child, grieving a loss, watching the news, fighting with a loved one, dreading the morning, not giving a crap about anything anymore, or whatever the case is—refocusing helps us look in a different direction. Refocusing helps us expand our perspective so we can expand ourselves.

If our response to an event produces messages that sound anything like this: "I'm not enough, I won't be able to handle it, I don't deserve happiness, I'm not allowed to have fun, resting is lazy, I'm not lovable, I don't belong, I'm never going to really succeed," it means that we're just not seeing everything. In the moment when we're triggered, we believe those messages declare our ultimate doom and destiny. They reinforce a narrative that probably developed during a traumatic event or a long time ago. But when we refocus, we trust that there's more to the story. When those messages become a focal point, we refocus to see more. Even if it makes your knees shake.

When we're skilled at refocusing, we notice the message and go beyond it by asking questions. "What's this *really* about and how might this very situation, which I'd rather not be in, actually be serving me? How might this moment be instructing me? How might this be a gift? What else is true? What information is missing?" Fulfillment doesn't happen in a straight line. Refocusing helps you befriend the detours.

Ultimately, refocusing relies on your ability to spontaneously and creatively leverage the inner skills you've been practicing. I encourage you to mash them up and make them your own. Customize them and evolve them. Pick out the bits that feel right, come back to any section when you need it, leave the rest. There are infinite ways for you to move through a tough spot. Refocusing relies on your ability to trust and choose what's appropriate for you in the moment. It relies on the idea that you are exactly where you need to be. It relies on the certainty that even when you don't know, you'll be guided back to your knowing. Refocusing is controlling what you can and surrendering to the rest. It's self-reliance that cooperates with the universe.

You have everything you need to refocus and get back Home to yourself. And getting there might be easier than you think. In *The Wizard of Oz*, all Dorothy needed to do was click her heels to return to Kansas. Let's review the inner skills and tools you've picked up along this yellow brick road.

Resilience: How to Manage Your Mind and Mood

In Chapter 1, we addressed dealing with setbacks by beginning with a practice of self-compassion. Self-compassion is a looking inward that involves labeling your emotion, being gentle with yourself, and reminding yourself that you're human and that suffering like this is universal. We discussed how resisting suffering actually makes it persist. Starting here sets you up for more ease because it helps you metabolize the issue without attacking yourself.

Beware of the trap of complaining because it exacerbates your negativity bias and blinds you to what's good. Take a Complaint Vacation and supplement with gratitude to make sure you're not only focusing on what's wrong but also on what's right.

If your inner critic sounds too loud with those doom and gloom messages, speak back with learned optimism: "What happened is not *personal*; it doesn't define me. It won't last forever; it's not *permanent*. What happened affects just one of many goals; it's not *pervasive* and spilling into every aspect of my career and life."

Check in on your Boring Basics, healthful things you know to do but can easily skip: deep breathing, optimal sleep, diet, hydration, movement, meditation, time in nature, and connection. When these are off balance, you are more vulnerable to being triggered and might have a harder time staying in command.

Clarity: How to Know What You Really, Really Want and Define Your Unique Vision of Success

Sometimes we get trapped by comparing ourselves to others. In Chapter 2, you created your unique vision to get clarity on who you are when you're most alive. We discussed the common pitfall of defining success in the usual backward way of first focusing on what you want to achieve. Instead, the key is to start by identifying how you want to feel and be and then to choose goals that align with that.

Read your vision, update it, hold it close when you feel yourself wandering astray or looking outside yourself to track how you're doing. Plug in to the sensations of what you're like in optimal conditions and let that be the focal point that draws you forward and inspires your goals.

Purpose: How to Make Conscious Decisions with Confidence and Live Your Values Every Day

When you're stuck, reflect on the accountability questions for your values and notice how you're actually being the person you want to be—even to the smallest degree. It's still enough to signal movement and to propel you even further.

In Chapter 3, you went through the Truth Organizer, a step-by-step process to articulate your values, which serve as guardrails for your decisions. Use your values to guide your choices, especially if you're feeling unsure of what to do, lost, or like nothing much matters. These guardrails keep you moving in the right lane so you make your way toward your vision. The accountability questions you developed are there so you can check in every day and celebrate your small wins. Progress—in any amount—is motivating and worth celebrating.

When you appreciate the conscious actions you're taking that align with your vision and values, you participate in a Virtuous Trifecta that yields organic confidence. You witness yourself influencing your reality, and that demonstrates that you do have control, even if things feel out of control. Looking back helps you move forward. Progress begets more progress.

Boundaries: How to Self-Care and Avoid Burnout

If it's a struggle to stay aligned with your values, boundaries can help. In Chapter 4, you used the Boundary Builder to identify how to create more ease in being who you want to be. Boundaries don't just keep things out but they amplify what you want to keep in. What value do you want to bolster and which experiences or activities will help you achieve that?

Set boundaries as modifications in a relationship, your schedule, your thinking, your space, or a process to have more of the experience that brings you alive. Remember that saying no is saying yes to something more important. If you've spent your life as a people pleaser, setting boundaries may feel uncomfortable, but that doesn't mean it's wrong. Be patient as your nervous system rewires itself to not automatically prioritize everyone else's needs above your well-being.

Play: How to Deal with Uncertainty

In Chapter 5, we discussed how uncertainty can trigger anxiety but also can generate excitement. To stay grounded and make better decisions in the face of the unknown, activate your playful mindset with the PLAY model and nudge your nervous system toward safety. PLAY doesn't have to happen in such a linear fashion as listed here; this is to help you remember the components:

- Pause and give yourself permission to see the situation differently.
- Let go of expectations and how it should go.
- Acknowledge your feelings.
- Say "Yes, and..." to accept the present moment for whatever it is and then to create the next choice for yourself.

When you're in a playful mindset, you can reframe a situation. Instead of feeling weighed down by obligation with a sense of "I have to," consider the opportunity in the situation with an "I get to" attitude.

Instead of dreading an event and predicting how bad it will be with "this is going to suck," approach it with curiosity: "I wonder how I might be surprised." Instead of complaining about what's wrong, notice what's right. Instead of feeling alone, notice how supported you are.

Discovery: How to Explore New Roles and Responsibilities

When you're feeling out of choices or don't like your options, turn to the exploration tools in Chapter 6. Consider how you can customize your role, or job craft, to feel more fulfilled—especially if you're dancing with the possibility of quitting. You can job craft your relationships, responsibilities, or how you relate to your work. To figure out what to shift, consider the following:

- Try something new and just call it an "experiment" to give yourself permission to feel it out before committing.
- If there's a role, team, or career that excites you, consider immersing yourself in it to learn more—can you shadow someone or take on a side project?
- Include others in your exploration by leading the learning—consider hosting a podcast or an event or writing a newsletter on themes you're interested in.
- Go on a Discovery Tour and conduct strategic informational interviews.
- Talk to your boss—sometimes a quick conversation can reveal the information you've been seeking. Do you need guidance, fuller feedback, clarity on your role, a sense of your growth opportunities? Ask for it directly.
- Give your mind and body space to relax. Let your default mode network do its thing and see what comes to you in the shower, while you're gardening, when you're out for a walk, or while doing laundry. Let yourself wander.

Approach: How to Transform Confrontations into Conversations

When you're stuck in passive-aggressive madness, feeling shut down, scared to speak up, or frustrated with someone, or you just don't know how to begin a difficult conversation, start with your approach. When it comes to difficult conversations, the most challenging part is the work you do before you speak. It starts with shifting your energy before you even talk. Because our emotions are contagious, your mood may say more than your words.

You want your approach to be conversational, signaling trust, not confrontational, signaling threat. Sort your story by framing a win-win intention, then specify the facts of what happened that upset you, what you felt as a consequence, and what foundational need was disrupted. Finish by proposing a new future you'd like to cocreate. Stay in empathy as you listen for the other person's experience.

Let's Get Meta: The Process of Writing This Book Has Been a Giant Practice in Refocusing

I started writing this book nine years ago, in 2014, when I was pregnant with my first child, Linor. I thought I'd finish the book proposal before she was born. A book proposal tells potential publishers what you plan to write and includes a sample chapter. It sounded like a reasonable and attainable goal at the time. But I had morning sickness and could barely peel myself off the couch. Whatever I had left to give was focused on growing my business so I could save up for my own maternity leave (self-employment!). Then it was time to adjust to being a new mom and not sleeping. Then we moved cross-country with a toddler. I tried not to let excuses get in my way. But I had to keep choosing the life in front of me. I did the smart goals. I calendared blank space to write. I hired a coach. I did all the right things you're supposed to do, but I barely inched along.

When I would get knocked off course, I stayed down to refocus. It wasn't pretty. I evaluated my choices. I asked what life was trying to tell me. I didn't like the answer: it was saying *not yet*. For years I pretended not to hear that message. I'd find myself squeezing water out of a stone. I'd spend my writing time looking blankly at the screen, going in circles, or marathoning on Netflix. I gave myself compassion: of course I was tired; anyone would be. I used my top value of Vitality to guide me, and I'd reluctantly choose to put my book to the side, for another day, another week, another year—so many times. I kept fighting, just like they tell you to do. Yet I kept getting pinned to the floor. What pissed me off was my willingness and desire to write paired with the knowingness that it just wasn't the right time. I worried I wasn't worthy of my dream to write a book.

To quell my insecurity, I used my accountability questions to stay steady and see that I was indeed experiencing my vision even without being published: I was taking care of my well-being, I was in loving relationships, I was in service to my clients. I was being the person I wanted to be. Yet my inner critic didn't stop nagging me about how much more I had left to do on the book proposal. I felt embarrassed that I had yet to reach that first milestone in becoming an author. I spoke back (sometimes yelled or cried back) to my inner critic with learned optimism. I'd remind myself that my delay wasn't permanent—I still had time. This wasn't personal, and it didn't mean I was a failure because I hadn't finished yet. And it wasn't pervasive because my business and family were flourishing.

On December 20, 2021, seven years in, I had dragged my way to being about 85 percent finished with my book proposal. I had one big final push left. And that's when I got punched in the gut. My goal was to complete the proposal before my surgery (the *BRCA*-related one), which was scheduled in early February. That gave me a little over a month before I hit instant menopause and God knows what life would be like. I planned to go away for a few days to finish the proposal. If I didn't, I feared that yet another year would slip by, again.

I stayed up late to pack my bags. I woke up early to nurse my baby. My husband moved his work around to support me. I had coffee in hand and opened the garage door with the other. That's when I got the call that my grandmother Raya had died. WTF. I was slammed into disbelief, sadness, and anger. I let out a huge primal scream. I closed the garage, threw my bags down, and cried. THAT'S IT!

This is when I refocused by letting go. I surrendered my space to create and opted to grieve instead. I was doing everything right, but it just wasn't the right time. We're called to refocus especially when we do everything right and still things go wrong.

Six weeks later, I went into surgery, got menopause, and it wasn't that bad. In fact, I was in awe of how graceful the entire experience turned out. I refocused by noticing the beauty in each encounter and let gratitude steer my attention. We arrived to the hospital with no traffic. The security guard who greeted us was named Angel. My waiting room had floor-to-ceiling windows overlooking a sparkling Queensboro Bridge. The sky reminded me of sherbet and glowed kindly at me. My surgeon said everything went flawlessly and I had one less incision than expected. Menopause is okay. I'm still myself. I couldn't lift my one-year-old son for six weeks, but I was still able to breastfeed while seated. Yep, I had menopause and could still breastfeed! The human body is amazing. Science is amazing. With a playful mindset, I welcomed the awe of my experience and stayed present to healing. I let myself consciously forget about the book proposal. My inner critic stayed quiet. Occasionally, when I'd remember and get the urge to plan my next step, I stopped myself. I got curious instead: "I wonder what will happen?"

I can't recall how or when, but one day I got the message "I'm ready." That last push, what I'd struggled to finish for seven years, just flowed out of me in about three weeks. I reconnected with an agent I had spoken with years ago and prayed she'd be willing to look at my work. Within a month, I had competing offers for a book deal.

The Work Happiness Method is about owning your power and controlling what you can; at the same time it's about acknowledging that maybe the parts you can't control are in service to you, too. I had so many existential wrestling matches. I didn't refocus without resistance. I was pinned down—again and again. It was ugly. But this process taught me it's safe to let go. It's safe to surrender. The message I got about "not yet" was right on. They say you can't give up. You better get back up when you fall down. But refocusing kept teaching me to fuck trying to be so good, so right, so hardworking. We all have different lessons, and that one may not be yours. But if you refocus, you'll sense what is.

During the seven years I felt stalled on my book proposal, I grew my business to a global level. I went from delivering one webinar to thirty people from my dining-room table to speaking to over fifty thousand people a year. The Work Happiness Method coaching program went from being my personal way out of hell to helping people from San Francisco, Egypt, and Qatar to Ghana, Singapore, Mexico, and Idaho. When I started my business, corporations were afraid of the word *happiness* and I had to use other words in my talks. After the Great Resignation, I no longer have to hide what I'm really trying to do. Who could have predicted a seismic shift in how people relate to their work? The most beautiful part of this process is the validation that it was happening perfectly—even the parts I thought were fucked. I was supported to arrive at this exact moment. I felt my grandmother and all my ancestors cheering for me.

This skill has been the hardest for me to learn and share. It's giving language to what doesn't have language. It requires brave listening to something intangible. It's awareness that comes through like a soft breeze. It relies on paying attention to subtlety and noticing what you notice, even if it's not what you want to acknowledge. The right answer won't always slap you in the face. It may come as a whisper or a hint.

Refocusing is trusting that growth is inevitable and being optimistic that it will work out. Patience and trust are two sides of the same coin. If it hasn't worked out for you, maybe it just hasn't worked out *yet*. The time between now and then is not wasted, it's nutritive. We don't judge a tree for being bare during winter. Even though it looks like nothing is stirring, miraculous preparation is happening below ground, readying it for an awesome burst of blossoms at just the right time. Flourishing is always in the works for us, and we don't have to always push so hard for it. Even when things don't flower as planned or they die off, those parts become fertilizer for the earth, transferring energy back to beget further growth. What if the very experience you feel holds you back is feeding your future?

Refocusing Practice

If you could use some support getting unstuck and returning to what's important, try the exercises below. Before you begin, put your hand on your heart. Take three deep, slow breaths.

▶ Recall a difficult experience that resulted in your growth. List all the ways you've directly or indirectly benefited.

_____

_____

_____

_____

▶ Now imagine a loving and kind wizard who only wants the best for you. This wizard is able to travel through both space and time. This means they can see a scenario from

(continues)

(continued)

thousands of feet up in the atmosphere, and they can get close enough to penetrate someone's mind and heart. The wizard has the ability to pop into the future and into the past. They can relay messages.

What caring message would you like the wizard to send to your past self, the self who went through the difficult experience?

_____

_____

_____

_____

► Now identify a current area, if you have one, where you feel offtrack or stuck or are experiencing resistance. Write down what's troubling you:

_____

_____

_____

_____

► Ask the wizard some questions and notice what answers pop up. Capture them without editing.

1. What's this situation *really* about and how might it actually be serving me?

_____

_____

_____

_____

2. How might this moment be instructing me?

_____

_____

_____

_____

3. How might this moment be a gift?

_____

_____

_____

_____

4. What else is true?

_____

_____

_____

_____

5. What information have I resisted acknowledging?

_____

_____

(continues)

(continued)

_____

_____

6. What additional information do I need in order to see the best possible outcome?

_____

_____

_____

_____

7. Which skills, tools, and resources might I use to relax into the offering?

_____

_____

_____

_____

▶ Perhaps the wizard senses you're not ready for the answer. If that's the case, trust that they'll reveal the answer at the right time. In the meanwhile, what's a way you can care for yourself?

_____

_____

_____

_____

It's Been for You, for All of Us

Even though technology is making some things easier, life seems harder. With escalating environmental disasters, economic and political instability, social injustice, mass shootings, extremism, hate crimes, and loneliness, it's challenging to focus on what's right when everything feels so wrong. Even if you're lucky and your small patch on this earth is safe, the people in your life are healthy, and your needs are covered, it's still tough to escape existential worry. That's because we're all interconnected. We mourn when others mourn, even if they're thousands of miles away, even when they are strangers, even when they are different. We know this on a cellular level. But just enough stress, distance, and busyness causes us to forget how together we are.

If we can be brought down by the unraveling of the world, we can also be lifted up, even by just one person. That's why this inner work of building your inner skills is vital. It's not just about you or me but about all of us. The beauty of our humanness is that we're designed to share. Without conscious effort, our nervous systems automatically know to work together, to co-regulate, and help us arrive at homeostasis, a balanced state. We need each other's care, not only to cope but also to live and be happy. The quality of our relationships is the biggest predictor of our happiness.[1] In the face of artificial intelligence, our connection to ourselves and each other becomes the authentic knowingness we can harness and further develop. Our human beingness is a sacred asset. When we do this work, we uplift each other. Possibilities unlock, potential is unleashed.

If you've been feeling squashed by the weight of the world, check your posture. When you get into alignment with yourself—by using your values, striving for your vision, maintaining healthy boundaries, staying light in the midst of uncertainty, exploring possibilities rather than contracting, opening to understand rather than judging—you automatically relieve your load. Because we're interlocked, we naturally shoulder things together. Someone makes pizzas, someone sells stationery, someone fixes dishwashers, someone cares for babies, someone organizes volunteers to build a playground, someone invents biodegradable plastic, someone heals wounds, someone grows cucumbers, someone writes laws. We're designed to work happier and live better *together*.

When you practice your inner skills and feel more fulfilled, it transcends your experience and cascades to those around you. It spontaneously affects how you greet a stranger in the elevator, how you phrase an email to your client, how you show interest in a child's story, how you have compassion for a friend, and how you forgive a loved one. When we have strong inner skills, it's easier to participate in the abundance of all the good things that matter. I once heard someone say, "When you find your piece in the puzzle, you enable ten thousand others to find theirs." The by-product of enhancing your inner skills is actually the end product you've been seeking all along: true fulfillment.

Fulfillment, or meaningful success, comes from contributing beyond ourselves and belonging to something bigger. It's not about us feeling better alone. Yes, the Work Happiness Method is about elevating yourself, but it's for the sake of us all. We can't help the world and be on purpose by abandoning ourselves; we each have to dip into our own aliveness first and let that source the rest. How wonderful that we're entrenched in a system of abundant flourishing...if we choose it. If we take responsibility for it.

I Believe in You

No need to climb a mountain to be inspired to succeed—you already are the very sight worth reveling in.

Mastering these inner skills for career fulfillment doesn't mean we're perfect, enlightened, or have arrived. It means we're becoming efficient in returning to ourselves with kindness, knowing what's true for ourselves in the moment, and steering ourselves toward growth. Your inner skills are there for you in any situation. We spend most of our waking hours at our jobs, so those interactions tend to be the sandpaper we need to smooth our edges. The stuff that brings us down can help us shine more brightly. Our light is then cast on our team, our families, the grocery store clerk, the barista, the stranger in the elevator.

I hope the Work Happiness Method has helped you. Writing this book for you has been an honor. Thank you for your time and willingness to read it. Please keep in touch and share what you've noticed. Email me at stella@workhappinessmethod.com, visit stellagrizont .com, or find me occasionally on some social media sites.

May you be healthy, happy, free to be yourself, safe, and know how loved you are. I believe in you.

Warmly,
Stella

Following are at-a-glance outlines that recap what you learned throughout this text.

Chapter 1: Resilience: How to Manage Your Mind and Mood

We have a negativity bias and can easily fall into mental traps of complaining and criticism. That keeps us stuck and sabotages our happiness and success at work. When you're having a tough moment, here are the tools to help manage your experience:

- **Self-compassion:** Label the emotion, remind yourself you're not the only one, be gentle.
- **Gratitude:** Write down three things you're grateful for each day.
- **Learned optimism:** It's not personal, it's not permanent, it's not pervasive.
- **Boring Basics:** Optimize for at least seven hours of sleep, maintain steady blood sugar levels, hydrate, move, exhale deeply, spend time in nature, and really connect with other people.

Chapter 2: Clarity: How to Know What You Really, Really Want and Define Your Unique Vision of Success

When it comes to defining success, beware of the third mental trap, comparison. Instead of gauging your level of success by comparing how you stack up to others or going outside yourself to judge how well you're doing, focus on your unique vision. Your vision is not a statement of things you wish to do but an expression of who you're being when you're most alive. Do the Vision Generator exercise.

Chapter 3: Purpose: How to Make Conscious Decisions with Confidence and Live Your Values Every Day

Values are the guideposts that influence your thoughts, decisions, and actions to move you toward your vision. They keep you in the right lane. Here are the steps to using the Truth Organizer:

- Do a messy brain dump and capture ten to fifteen desired qualities, attributes, sensations, or strengths you'd like to embody.
- Clean up your list by consolidating redundancies.
- Define each term or phrase.
- Title your values.
- Rank your values to help you prioritize which to choose when there's a conflict.
- Rate the degree to which you're experiencing each value currently (1–100 percent).
- Identify three values you want to focus on amplifying right away.
- Design accountability questions that help you do a quick check-in on those values each day.

VIRTUOUS TRIFECTA

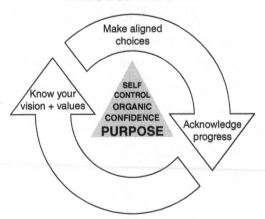

By practicing your accountability questions and noticing your progress, you participate in a Virtuous Trifecta. Your awareness of your values-aligned actions begets more of the same. This gives way to organic confidence and a purposeful life.

Chapter 4: Boundaries: How to Self-Care and Avoid Burnout
Boundaries aren't just a matter of saying no. In fact, boundaries are saying yes to what's important. Boundaries better enable you to express your values and operate with greater freedom, security, and ease. In this way, they help you prevent burnout because you maintain integrity with yourself and what matters.

- Use the Energy Inventory Tracker to evaluate how you spend your time and energy and regain spaciousness in your schedule, relationships, and mind.
- Use the Boundary Builder to figure out where to set those boundaries.
  - What value, feeling, or strength do you want to experience more of?
  - What activity would make it easier for you to experience that value, feeling, or strength?
  - Consider these thought starters as potential spots to place boundaries:
    - Relationships: Which interactions do you need to start, stop, increase, or decrease?
    - Time: What do you need to change about your schedule?
    - Beliefs: How can you choose a better belief?
    - Systematizing: What can you automate to reduce how much you have to think and choose?
    - Environment: How can you modify your space to better support you?

Chapter 5: Play: How to Deal with Uncertainty

Our reality is subjective. Our brain perceives what's true in the moment on the basis of limited data points and is influenced by past experiences, our mood, and our sense of safety. Our experience of uncertainty runs on a continuum. Depending on how safe we feel, we perceive the uncertainty as anxiety-provoking or exciting. Actively marshaling a playful mindset helps shift anxiety over the unknown into a willingness to explore possibilities instead of shutting down.

RESPONSE TO THE UNKNOWN
A CONTINUUM

To reframe your experience of the unknown, use the four steps to PLAY:

1. **Pause** and give yourself permission to see the situation differently.
2. **Let** go of expectations and how it should go.
3. **Acknowledge** your feelings.
4. Say **"Yes, and…"** to accept the present moment for what it is and to create the next choice for yourself.

Chapter 6: Discovery: How to Explore New Roles and Responsibilities

The key to figuring out what's next is gathering information and then filtering it through your values and vision. Here's how to gather the data points you need:

- Try something new and just call it an "experiment" to give yourself permission to feel it out before committing.

- If there's a role, team, or career that excites you, consider immersing yourself in it to learn more—can you shadow someone or take on a side project?
- You could also include others in your exploration by leading the learning—consider publishing a podcast, hosting events, or writing a newsletter on themes you're interested in.
- Go on a Discovery Tour and conduct strategic informational interviews.
- Talk to your boss—sometimes a quick conversation reveals the information you've been seeking. Do you need guidance, fuller feedback, clarity on your role, a sense of your growth opportunities? Ask for it directly.
- Give your mind and body space to relax. Let your default mode network do its thing and see what comes to you in the shower, while you're gardening, when you're out for a walk, or while doing the laundry. Let yourself wander.

Chapter 7: Approach: How to Transform Confrontations into Conversations

Your approach represents the energy you give off as you move toward another person. Your energy matters more than your words because emotions are contagious. Your approach can signal safety, openness, and willingness to have a conversation, or it can signal threat and make the other person feel like this is a confrontation. Here are the differences between confrontation mode and conversation mode:

	Confrontation Mode	Conversation Mode
Objective	To battle, persuade, or command	To share understanding
Outlook	Convinced	Curious
Emotional state	Pessimistic	Optimistic

	Confrontation Mode	Conversation Mode
Body	Unsafe: Stress hormones	Safe: Oxytocin release
Relationship	Me versus them	Us
Tempo	Escalating	Deescalating
Options	Limited: A or B	Emerging possibilities
Outcome	Winner and loser or loser and loser	Transformation

Prepare these three parts—the Three Ss—to maintain a conversational approach:

1. Shift your energy—downregulate your nervous system so you can authentically be curious and open. This means you may have to delay the conversation.

2. Sort your story with the Five Fs—slow down to get clear on what happened and what you're hoping for:
   a. Frame: What's the win-win intention?
   b. Facts: What specifically happened that upset you?
   c. Feeling: How did you feel and what was the consequence of your feeling that way?
   d. Foundation: What value, condition, or desire was compromised that's essential for your comfort, well-being, or optimal performance?
   e. Future: What specific actions would support your foundation and fit into the frame?

3. Stay in empathy—be willing to see things differently and from the other person's perspective.

Chapter 8: Refocus: How to Return to What Matters (Without Pushing So Hard)

To refocus means to return to yourself and what matters when you inevitably hit a setback, get derailed, feel stuck, or are lost. Refocusing is a willingness to see an obstacle not only for what it blocks but also for what it opens. It's about expanding our perspective so we can expand ourselves. Ultimately, refocusing relies on your ability to spontaneously and creatively leverage the inner skills you've been practicing. I encourage you to mash them up and make them your own. Customize them and evolve them. When you find yourself in a situation you'd rather not be in, ask yourself these questions:

- What's this situation *really* about and how might it actually be serving me?
- How might this moment be instructing me?
- How might this moment be a gift?
- What else is true?
- What information have I resisted acknowledging?
- What additional information do I need in order to see a beautiful, loving, perfect outcome?
- Which skills, tools, and resources might I use to relax into the offering?

My work has been inspired by a lot of books and people. If you want to keep learning, here's a place to start, sorted by category. If I've made a mistake in my attributions or a new study updates findings that I've shared, I'd appreciate hearing from you. My email address is stella@workhappinessmethod.com.

Achievement

Big Potential: How Transforming the Pursuit of Success Raises Our Achievement, Happiness, and Well-Being by Shawn Achor

Everything Is Figureoutable by Marie Forleo

Grit: The Power of Passion and Perseverance by Angela Duckworth

Mindset: The New Psychology of Success by Carol S. S. Dweck

Rethinking Positive Thinking: Inside the New Science of Motivation by Gabriele Oettingen

Rise of Superman: Decoding the Science of Ultimate Human Performance by Steven Kotler

The Willpower Instinct: How Self-Control Works, Why It Matters, and What You Can Do to Get More of It by Kelly McGonigal

Boundaries, Burnout, Stress, and Trauma

Burnout: The Secret to Unlocking the Stress Cycle by Emily Nagoski and Amelia Nagoski

No Bad Parts: Healing Trauma and Restoring Wholeness with the Internal Family Systems Model by Richard Schwartz

The Pocket Guide to the Polyvagal Theory: The Transformative Power of Feeling Safe by Stephen W. Porges

Set Boundaries, Find Peace: A Guide to Reclaiming Yourself by Nedra Glover Tawwab

When the Body Says No: Exploring the Stress-Disease Connection by Gabor Maté

Communication and Connection

Braving the Wilderness: The Quest for True Belonging and the Courage to Stand Alone by Brené Brown

Friend and Foe: When to Cooperate, When to Compete, and How to Succeed at Both by Adam Galinsky

Love 2.0: Creating Happiness and Health in Moments of Connection by Barbara Fredrickson

Never Split the Difference: Negotiating As If Your Life Depended on It by Chris Voss, with Tahl Raz

Nonviolent Communication: A Language of Life: Life-Changing Tools for Healthy Relationships by Marshall B. Rosenberg

Radical Candor: Be a Kick-Ass Boss Without Losing Your Humanity by Kim Scott

Creativity, Play, and Uncertainty

Flow: The Psychology of Optimal Experience by Mihaly Csikszentmihalyi

Play: How It Shapes the Brain, Opens the Imagination, and Invigorates the Soul by Stuart Brown and Christopher Vaughan

Sprint: How to Solve Big Problems and Test New Ideas in Just Five Days by Jake Knapp

Think Again: The Power of Knowing What You Don't Know by Adam Grant

Happiness, Resilience, and Self-Compassion

Flourish: A Visionary New Understanding of Happiness and Well-Being by Martin E. P. Seligman

The Happiness Advantage: How a Positive Brain Fuels Success in Work and Life by Shawn Achor

Learned Optimism: How to Change Your Mind and Your Life by Martin E. P. Seligman

Positivity: Discover the Upward Spiral That Will Change Your Life by Barbara Fredrickson

Profit from the Positive: Proven Leadership Strategies to Boost Productivity and Transform Your Business by Margaret Greenberg and Senia Maymin

Resilient Grieving: How to Find Your Way Through a Devastating Loss (Finding Strength and Embracing Life After a Loss That Changes Everything) by Lucy Hone

Self-Compassion: The Proven Power of Being Kind to Yourself by Kristin Neff

Healthy Habits (aka the Boring Basics)

Breath: The New Science of a Lost Art by James Nestor

Forest Bathing: How Trees Can Help You Find Health and Happiness by Qing Li

In the FLO: Unlock Your Hormonal Advantage and Revolutionize Your Life by Alisa Vitti

The Joy of Movement: How Exercise Helps Us Find Happiness, Hope, Connection, and Courage by Kelly McGonigal

Mindfulness for Beginners by Jon Kabat-Zinn

Outlive: The Science and Art of Longevity by Peter Attia

Smarter Not Harder: The Biohacker's Guide to Getting the Body and Mind You Want by Dave Asprey

The Whole30: The 30-Day Guide to Total Health and Food Freedom by Melissa Hartwig, Dallas Hartwig, and Melissa Urban

Why We Sleep: Unlocking the Power of Sleep and Dreams by Matthew Walker

Purpose, Values, and Vision

The Book of Awakening: Having the Life You Want by Being Present to the Life You Have by Mark Nope

A New Earth: Awakening to Your Life's Purpose by Eckhart Tolle

The Way of Integrity: Finding the Path to Your True Self by Martha Beck

Meaning, Spirituality, and Transcendence

Awe: The New Science of Everyday Wonder and How It Can Transform Your Life by Dacher Keltner

Broken Open: How Difficult Times Help Us Grow by Elizabeth Lesser

Man's Search for Meaning by Viktor E. Frankl

The Power of Awe: Overcome Burnout and Anxiety, Ease Chronic Pain, Find Clarity and Purpose—In Less Than One Minute Per Day by Jake Eagle and Michael Amster

Seven Thousand Ways to Listen: Staying Close to What Is Sacred by Mark Nepo

Tears to Triumph: The Spiritual Journey from Suffering to Enlightenment by Marianne Williamson

Transcend: The New Science of Self-Actualization by Scott Barry Kauffman

Introduction: The Eight Inner Skills

1 Gallup, "State of the Global Workplace: 2023 Report," www.gallup.com/workplace/349484/state-of-the-global-workplace.aspx.

2 Acumen Research and Consulting, "Soft Skills Training Market Size Will Achieve USD 66,075 Million by 2030 Growing at 12.2% CAGR—Exclusive Report by Acumen Research and Consulting," GlobeNewswire, August 22, 2022, www.globenewswire.com/en/news-release/2022/08/22/2502574/0/en/Soft-Skills-Training-Market-Size-Will-Achieve-USD-66-075-Million-by-2030-growing-at-12-2-CAGR-Exclusive-Report-by-Acumen-Research-and-Consulting.html.

3 Jacques Bughin, Eric Hazan, Susan Lund, Peter Dahlström, Anna Wiesinger, and Amresh Subramaniam, "Skill Shift: Automation and the Future of the Workforce," McKinsey & Company, May 23, 2018, www.mckinsey.com/featured-insights/future-of-work/skill-shift-automation-and-the-future-of-the-workforce.

4 Martin E. P. Seligman, *Flourish: A Visionary New Understanding of Happiness and Well-Being* (New York: Free Press, 2011).

5 E. Diener and R. Biswas-Diener, *Happiness: Unlocking the Mysteries of Psychological Wealth* (Malden, MA: Wiley/Blackwell, 2008).

Chapter 1: Resilience: How to Manage Your Mind and Mood

1 A. Ledgerwood and A. E. Boydstun, "Sticky Prospects: Loss Frames Are Cognitively Stickier Than Gain Frames," *Journal of Experimental Psychology: General* 143, no. 1 (2014): 376–385, https://doi.org/10.1037/a0032310.

2 Timothy D. Wilson, *Strangers to Ourselves: Discovering the Adaptive Unconscious* (Cambridge, MA: Belknap Press, 2002).

3 Shawn Achor, *Before Happiness: The 5 Hidden Keys to Achieving Success, Spreading Happiness, and Sustaining Positive Change* (New York: Crown, 2013).

4 Marcel Proust, *In Search of Lost Time: Volume 1 of Á La Recherche Du Temps Perdu*, Marcel Proust Modern Library Classics (New York: Random House, 2003).

5 Heather A. Wadlinger and Derek M. Isaacowitz, "Positive Mood Broadens Visual Attention to Positive Stimuli," *Motivation and Emotion* 30, no. 1 (2006): 87–99, https://doi.org/10.1007/s11031-006-9021-1.

6 K. D. Vohs, B. D. Glass, W. T. Maddox, and A. B. Markman, "Ego Depletion Is Not Just Fatigue: Evidence from a Total Sleep Deprivation Experiment," *Social Psychological and Personality Science* 2, no. 2 (2010): 166, https://doi.org/10.1177/1948550610386123; Harvard Health Publishing, "Giving Thanks Can Make You Happier," August 14, 2021, www.health.harvard.edu/healthbeat/giving-thanks-can-make-you-happier.

7 Kristin Neff, *Self-Compassion: The Proven Power of Being Kind to Yourself* (New York: William Morrow, 2011).

8 Matthew D. Lieberman, Naomi I. Eisenberger, Molly J. Crockett, Sabrina M. Tom, Jennifer H. Pfeifer, and Baldwin M. Way, "Putting Feelings into Words: Affect Labeling Disrupts Amygdala Activity in Response to Affective Stimuli," *Psychological Science* 18, no. 5 (2007): 421–428, www.jstor.org/stable/40064633.

9 Will Bowen, *A Complaint Free World: How to Stop Complaining and Start Enjoying the Life You Always Wanted* (New York: Three Rivers Press, 2013).

10 Sigal G. Barsade and Donald E. Gibson, "Why Does Affect Matter in Organizations?" *Academy of Management Perspectives* 21, no. 1 (2007): 36–59, https://doi.org/10.5465/AMP.2007.24286163.

11 Robert A. Emmons and Michael E. McCullough, "Counting Blessings Versus Burdens: An Experimental Investigation of Gratitude and Subjective Well-Being in Daily Life," *Journal of Personality and Social Psychology* 84, no. 2 (2003): 377–389, https://doi.org/10.1037/0022-3514.84.2.377.

12 Martin E. P. Seligman, T. A. Steen, N. Park, and C. Peterson, "Positive Psychology Progress: Empirical Validation of Interventions," *American Psychologist* 60, no. 5 (2005): 410–421, https://doi.org/10.1037/0003-066X.60.5.410.

13 B. J. Fogg, *Tiny Habits: The Small Changes That Change Everything* (Boston: Houghton Mifflin Harcourt, 2020).

14 Martin E. P. Seligman, *Learned Optimism: How to Change Your Mind and Your Life* (New York: Vintage, 2006).

15 James Nestor, *Breath: The New Science of a Lost Art* (New York: Riverhead Books, 2020).

16 Melis Y. Balban, Eric Neri, Manuela M. Kogon, Lara Weed, Bita Nouri-ani, Booil Jo, Gary Holl, Jamie M. Zeitzer, David Spiegel, and Andrew D. Huberman, "Brief Structured Respiration Practices Enhance Mood and Reduce Physiological Arousal," *Cell Reports Medicine* 4, no. 1 (2023): 100895, https://doi.org/10.1016/j.xcrm.2022.100895.

17 A. M. Williamson and Anne-Marie Feyer, "Moderate Sleep Deprivation Produces Impairments in Cognitive and Motor Performance Equivalent to Legally Prescribed Levels of Alcohol Intoxication," *Occupational and Environmental Medicine* 57, no. 10 (2000): 649–655, www.jstor.org/stable/27731389.

18 Arianna Huffington, *The Sleep Revolution: Transforming Your Life, One Night at a Time* (New York: Harmony, 2016); Matthew Walker, *Why We Sleep: Unlocking the Power of Sleep and Dreams* (New York: Scribner, 2018).

19 Fahimeh Haghighatdoost, Awat Feizi, Ahmad Esmaillzadeh, Nafiseh Rashidi-Pourfard, Ammar Hassanzadeh Keshteli, Hamid Roohafza, and Payman Adibi, "Drinking Plain Water Is Associated with Decreased Risk of Depression and Anxiety in Adults: Results from a Large Cross-sectional Study," *World Journal of Psychiatry* 8, no. 3 (2018): 88–96, https://doi.org/10.5498/wjp.v8.i3.88.

20 Raza Ahmad, "How Much Water Do You Need Each Day?" Health and Wellness (blog), Penn Medicine, May 20, 2015, https://www.pennmedicine.org/updates/blogs/health-and-wellness/2015/may/how-much-water-do-you-need-each-day.

21 Julia C. Basso and Wendy A. Suzuki, "The Effects of Acute Exercise on Mood, Cognition, Neurophysiology, and Neurochemical Pathways: A Review," *Brain Plasticity* 2 (2017): 127–152.

22 Carolyn Saarni, *The Development of Emotional Competence*, Guilford Series on Social and Emotional Development (New York: Guilford Press, 1999).

23 Yoshifumi Miyazaki, *Shinrin Yoku: The Japanese Art of Forest Bathing* (Portland, OR: Timber Press, 2018).

24 F. S. Mayer, Cynthia M. Frantz, Emma Bruehlman-Senecal, and Kyffin Dolliver, "Why Is Nature Beneficial?: The Role of Connectedness to Nature," *Environment and Behavior* 41, no. 5 (2008): 607–643, https://doi.org/10.1177/0013916508319745.

25 Kristine Engemann, Carsten Bøcker Pedersen, Lars Arge, Constantinos Tsirogiannis, Preben B. Mortensen, and Jens-Christian Svenning, "Residential Green Space in Childhood Is Associated with Lower Risk of Psychiatric Disorders from Adolescence into Adulthood," *Proceedings of the National Academy of Sciences of the United States of America* 116, no. 11 (2019): 5188–5193, https://doi.org/10.1073/pnas.1807504116.

26 Raelyne L. Dopko, Colin A. Capaldi, and John M. Zelenski, "The Psychological and Social Benefits of a Nature Experience for Children: A Preliminary Investigation," *Journal of Environmental Psychology* 63 (2019): 134–138, https://doi.org/10.1016/j.jenvp.2019.05.002.

27 Julianne Holt-Lunstad, Theodore Robles, and David A. Sbarra, "Advancing Social Connection as a Public Health Priority in the United States," *American Psychologist* 72, no. 6 (2017): 517–530, https://doi.org/10.1037/amp0000103.

28 Simone Schnall, Kent D. Harber, Jeanine K. Stefanucci, and Dennis R. Proffitt, "Social Support and the Perception of Geographical Slant," *Journal of Experimental Social Psychology* 44, no. 5 (2008): 1246–1255, https://doi.org/10.1016/j.jesp.2008.04.011.

29 Alok Patel and Stephanie Plowman, "The Increasing Importance of a Best Friend at Work," Gallup, August 17, 2022, www.gallup.com/workplace/397058/increasing-importance-best-friend-work.aspx.

30 Andrew Steptoe, Natalie Owen, Sabine R. Kunz-Ebrecht, and Lena Brydon, "Loneliness and Neuroendocrine, Cardiovascular, and Inflammatory Stress Responses in Middle-Aged Men and Women," *Psychoneuroendocrinology* 29, no. 5 (2004): 593–611, https://doi.org/10.1016/S0306-4530(03)00086-6.

31 Hanne K. Collins, Serena F. Hagerty, Jordi Quoidbach, Michael I. Norton, and Alison W. Brooks, "Relational Diversity in Social Portfolios Predicts Well-Being," *Proceedings of the National Academy of Sciences* 119, no. 43 (2022), https://www.pnas.org/doi/full/10.1073/pnas.2120668119.

Chapter 2: Clarity: How to Know What You Really, Really Want and Develop Your Unique Vision of Success

1   V. K. Ranganathan, V. Siemionow, J. Z. Liu, V. Sahgal, and G. H. Yue, "From Mental Power to Muscle Power—Gaining Strength by Using the Mind," *Neuropsychologia* 42, no. 7 (2004): 944–956, https://doi.org/10.1016/j.neuropsychologia.2003.11.018.

2   Niño Fredrico L. Narvacan, Evangeline Atienza-Bulaquiña, and Lucille D. Evangelista, "Effects of Visualization on Academic Performance of College Students," *International Journal of Information and Education Technology* 4, no. 2 (2014): 156–160, https://doi.org/10.7763/IJIET.2014.V4.389.

3   Jantine J. L. M. Boselie, Linda M. G. Vancleef, Susan van Hooren, and Madelon L. Peters, "The Effectiveness and Equivalence of Different Versions of a Brief Online Best Possible Self (BPS) Manipulation to Temporary Increase Optimism and Affect," *Journal of Behavior Therapy and Experimental Psychiatry* 79 (2023): 101837, https://doi.org/10.1016/j.jbtep.2023.101837.

Chapter 3: Purpose: How to Make Conscious Decisions with Confidence and Live Your Values Every Day

1 Geoffrey L. Cohen and David K. Sherman, "The Psychology of Change: Self-Affirmation and Social Psychological Intervention," *Annual Review of Psychology* 65 (2014): 333–371, https://doi.org/10.1146/annurev -psych-010213-115137.

2 Teresa Amabile and Steven Kramer, *The Progress Principle: Using Small Wins to Ignite Joy, Engagement, and Creativity at Work* (Cambridge, MA: Harvard Business Review Press, 2011).

3 Joseph C. Nunes and Xavier Drèze, "The Endowed Progress Effect: How Artificial Advancement Increases Effort," *Journal of Consumer Research* 32, no. 4 (2006): 504–512, https://doi.org/10.1086/500480.

4 Pauline R. Clance and Suzanne Imes, "The Imposter Phenomenon in High Achieving Women: Dynamics and Therapeutic Intervention," *Psychotherapy: Theory, Research, and Practice* 15, no. 3 (1978): 241–247, www.paulineroseclance.com/pdf/ip_high_achieving_women.pdf.

Chapter 4: Boundaries: How to Self-Care and Avoid Burnout

1 Pete Walker, *Complex PTSD: From Surviving to Thriving* (CreateSpace, 2013).

2 Nicole LePera, *How to Do the Work: Recognize Your Patterns, Heal from Your Past, and Create Your Self* (New York: Harper Wave, 2021); John Bowlby, *Attachment: Attachment and Loss*, vol. 1 (New York: Basic Books, 1969).

3 Regina Sullivan, Rosemarie Perry, Aliza Sloan, Karine Kleinhaus, and Nina Burtchen, "Infant Bonding and Attachment to the Caregiver: Insights from Basic and Clinical Science," *Clinics in Perinatology* 38, no. 4 (2011): 643–655, https://doi.org/10.1016/j.clp.2011.08.011.

4 Sullivan et al., "Infant Bonding and Attachment to the Caregiver," 643–655.

5 Stephen Porges, "What's Happening in the Nervous System of Patients Who 'Please and Appease' (or Fawn) in Response to Trauma?" National Institute for the Clinical Application of Behavioral Medicine, October 1, 2021, www.nicabm.com/working-with-please-and-appease/.

6 Lydia Saad, Sangeeta Agrawal, and Ben Wigert, "Gender Gap in Worker Burnout Widened Amid the Pandemic," Gallup, December 27, 2021, www.gallup.com/workplace/358349/gender-gap-worker-burnout -widened-amid-pandemic.aspx.

7 Gallup, *Gallup's Perspective on Employee Burnout: Causes and Cures* (Washington, DC: Gallup, 2020), www.gallup.com/workplace /282659/employee-burnout-perspective-paper.aspx?thank-you-report -form=1.

8 American Psychological Association, *Stress in America: Paying with Our Health* (Washington, DC: American Psychological Association, February 4, 2015), www.apa.org/news/press/releases/stress/2014/stress-report.pdf.

9 Gallup, *Gallup's Perspective on Employee Burnout*, www.gallup.com/workplace/282659/employee-burnout-perspective-paper.aspx?thank-you-report-form=1.

10 Arnold B. Bakker and Evangelia Demerouti, "The Job Demands-Resources Model: State of the Art," *Journal of Managerial Psychology* 22, no. 3 (2007): 309–328, https://doi.org/10.1108/02683940710733115.

11 Gabor Maté, *When the Body Says No: Exploring the Stress-Disease Connection* (New York: John Wiley & Sons, 2011).

12 M. Wirsching, H. Stierlin, F. Hoffmann, G. Weber, and B. Wirsching, "Psychological Identification of Breast Cancer Patients Before Biopsy," *Journal of Psychosomatic Research* 26, no. 1 (1982): 1–10, https://doi.org/10.1016/0022-3999(82)90057-5.

13 David M. Kissen and H. J. Eysenck, "Personality in Male Lung Cancer Patients," *Journal of Psychosomatic Research* 6, no. 2 (1962): 123–127, https://doi.org/10.1016/0022-3999(62)90062-4.

14 Emily Nagoski and Amelia Nagoski, *Burnout: The Secret to Unlocking the Stress Cycle* (New York: Ballantine Books, 2019).

15 D. J. Bem, "Self-Perception Theory," in *Advances in Experimental Social Psychology*, ed. L. Berkowitz, 1–62 (New York: Academic Press, 1972).

16 Gabriele Oettingen, *Rethinking Positive Thinking: Inside the New Science of Motivation* (New York: Penguin, 2014).

Chapter 5: Play: How to Deal with Uncertainty

1 Anil Seth, *Being You: A New Science of Consciousness* (New York: Dutton, 2021).

2 Amos Tversky and Daniel Kahneman, "Loss Aversion in Riskless Choice: A Reference-Dependent Model," *Quarterly Journal of Economics* 106, no. 4 (1991): 1039–1061, https://doi.org/10.2307/2937956.

3 Stephen W. Porges, *The Polyvagal Theory: Neurophysiological Foundations of Emotions, Attachment, Communication, and Self-Regulation* (New York: W. W. Norton, 2011).

4 Stephen W. Porges, "Play as a Neural Exercise: Insights from the Polyvagal Theory," Olive Branch Counseling and Training, https://olivebranchsa.com/portfolio-view/play-as-a-neural-exercise-insights-from-the-polyvagal-theory/.

5 Brian Sutton-Smith, *The Ambiguity of Play* (Cambridge, MA: Harvard University Press, 2009).

6   Stuart Brown and Christopher Vaughan, *Play: How It Shapes the Brain, Opens the Imagination, and Invigorates the Soul* (New York: Avery Publishing, 2009).

7   Chris Voss and Tahl Raz, *Never Split the Difference: Negotiating As If Your Life Depended on It* (New York: Harper Business Books, 2016).

8   Brown and Vaughan, *Play.*

9   Andrew N. Iwaniuk, J. E. Nelson, and S. M. Pellis, "Do Big-Brained Animals Play More? Comparative Analyses of Play and Relative Brain Size in Mammals," *Journal of Comparative Psychology* 115, no. 1 (2001): 29–41.

10 John Byers, "The Biology of Human Play," *Child Development* 69, no. 3 (2008): 599–600, https://doi.org/10.1111/j.1467-8624.1998.tb06227.x.

Chapter 6: Discovery: How to Explore New Roles and Responsibilities

1   J. M. Berg, J. E. Dutton, and A. Wrzesniewski, "Job Crafting and Meaningful Work," in *Purpose and Meaning in the Workplace*, ed. B. J. Dik, Z. S. Byrne, and M. F. Steger, 81–104 (Washington, DC: American Psychological Association, 2013), https://doi.org/10.1037/14183-005.

2   Roger E. Beaty, Mathias Benedek, Robin W. Wilkins, Emanuel Jauk, Andreas Fink, Paul J. Silvia, Donald A. Hodges, Karl Koschutnig, and Aljoscha C. Neubauer, "Creativity and the Default Network: A Functional Connectivity Analysis of the Creative Brain at Rest," *Neuropsychologia* 64 (2014): 92–98, https://doi.org/10.1016/j.neuropsychologia.2014.09.019.

3   Damien Newman, "The Design Squiggle," Design Squiggle, https://thedesignsquiggle.com/.

4   Mihaly Csikszentmihalyi, *Flow: The Psychology of Optimal Experience* (New York: Harper Perennial Modern Classics, 2008).

5   Angela Duckworth, *Grit: The Power of Passion and Perseverance* (New York: Scribner, 2016).

Chapter 7: Approach: How to Transform Confrontations into Conversations

1   Stephen W. Porges, *The Pocket Guide to the Polyvagal Theory: The Transformative Power of Feeling Safe* (New York: W. W. Norton, 2017).

2   Uri Hasson, Asif A. Ghazanfar, Bruno Galantucci, Simon Garrod, and Christian Keysers, "Brain-to-Brain Coupling: A Mechanism for Creating and Sharing a Social World," *Trends in Cognitive Sciences* 16, no. 2 (2012): 114–121, https://doi.org/10.1016/j.tics.2011.12.007.

3   Heenam Yoon, Sang H. Choi, Sang K. Kim, Hyun B. Kwon, Seong M. Oh, Jae-Won Choi, Yu J. Lee, Do-Un Jeong, and Kwang S. Park, "Human

Heart Rhythms Synchronize While Co-sleeping," *Frontiers in Physiology* 10 (2019): 190, https://doi.org/10.3389/fphys.2019.00190.

4 Kerstin Uvnäs-Moberg, Linda Handlin, and Maria Petersson, "Self-Soothing Behaviors with Particular Reference to Oxytocin Release Induced by Non-noxious Sensory Stimulation," *Frontiers in Psychology* 5 (2014): 1529, https://doi.org/10.3389/fpsyg.2014.01529.

5 Yuki Takayanagi and Tatsushi Onaka, "Roles of Oxytocin in Stress Responses, Allostasis and Resilience," *International Journal of Molecular Sciences* 23, no. 1 (2022): 150, https://doi.org/10.3390/ijms23010150.

6 Chris Argyris and Donald A. Schon, *Organizational Learning: A Theory of Action Perspective* (Boston: Addison-Wesley, 1978).

7 Marshall B. Rosenberg, *Nonviolent Communication: A Language of Life*, 2nd ed. (Encinitas, CA: PuddleDancer Press, 2003).

8 Cendri A. Hutcherson, Emma M. Seppala, and James J. Gross, "Loving-Kindness Meditation Increases Social Connectedness," *Emotion* 8, no. 5 (2008): 720–724, https://doi.org/10.1037/a0013237.

9 Matthieu Ricard, Antoine Lutz, and Richard J. Davidson, "Mind of the Meditator," *Scientific American* 311, no. 5 (2014): 38–45, https://doi.org/10.1038/scientificamerican1114-38.

10 Barbara L. Fredrickson, Michael A. Cohn, Kimberly A. Coffey, Jolynn Pek, and Sandra M. Finkel, "Open Hearts Build Lives: Positive Emotions, Induced Through Loving-Kindness Meditation, Build Consequential Personal Resources," *Journal of Personality and Social Psychology* 95, no. 5 (2008): 1045–1062, https://doi.org/10.1037/a0013262.

11 Chris Voss and Tahl Raz, *Never Split the Difference: Negotiating As If Your Life Depended on It* (New York: Harper Business Books, 2016).

12 Hasson et al., "Brain-to-Brain Coupling," 114–121.

Chapter 8: Refocus: How to Return to What Matters (Without Pushing So Hard)

1 Sally Maitlis, "Posttraumatic Growth at Work," *Annual Review of Organizational Psychology and Organizational Behavior* 7 (2020): 395–419, https://doi.org/10.1146/annurev-orgpsych-012119-044932.

Conclusion: It's Been for You, for All of Us

1 Robert Waldinger, "What Makes a Good Life? Lessons from the Longest Study on Happiness," video 12:38, TEDxBeaconStreet, TED, November 2015, https://www.ted.com/talks/robert_waldinger_what_makes_a_good_life_lessons_from_the_longest_study_on_happiness/c?language=en.

I've been looking forward to writing this part the most. And yet, now that I'm here, it feels impossible to come up with the right words and capture all the people. I didn't mention it earlier as a tool for generating happiness...but do this. Write a letter of thanks to everyone who helped get you to where you are. Like me, I'm sure you'll be flooded with gratitude and love. In many ways while writing this book, I felt like I was walking a treacherous path all alone. But now, as I wrap up and reflect deeply on who helped me get here, I realize just how held and supported I've been all along. This is a testament to togetherness.

I thank each client, team member, intern, vendor, friend, family member, colleague, publishing team member, and beyond. Each of our interactions has been important, so thank you for whoever has crossed my path; you're woven into this fabric. I'm sure that I'll look back and realize that I missed some critical names; for that, forgive me. My love flies to you all.

To My Family

To my husband, Ilya. Thank you for creating the space and giving me the grace to do this work and be myself. Thank you for cheering me on and loving me through all the moods and pages. From our first date, an immersive research project on play, to assembling my iScream Trucks, to giving me feedback despite my defensiveness, to 24/7 IT support, to fathering, you are my sandpaper and my cosmic comfort. The *nitichka* only gets stronger.

Thank you to my children, who deliver awe, joy, and hope each day. Linor, you've been my growth accelerator. Your love and existence have propelled me to do this work. Linor wants the world to know—and I agree—kids' feelings and needs deserve respect. Lev, thank you for reminding me to trust. Thank you for coming at just the right time to help me embody love and to encourage me to set boundaries. You both are my greatest teachers.

To my parents, who gave me my first job at their optical store. Mama, you inspire me to live life brightly, boldly, and beautifully. Thank you for always believing in me. I know your love, courage, and strength go deeper than I can fathom. Papa, thank you for your tender heart, care, wisdom, and for making us laugh. You always reinforce the truth: family matters. And your delicious *plov* brings us together!

To my sister Biana, thank you for being there—on a tightrope or in a tight spot, I'm grateful to have you in my life. You've supported me, from being my shopping assistant and my intern at the iScream Truck to helping launch the Work Happiness Method at organizations.

To my in-laws, Sonyachka and Fimachka, how did I get so lucky? I hope Ilya and I will have as rich a life as you when we reach your years—surrounded by friends, engaged in culture and passion, and walking four miles a day!

To my sister-in-law, Anya. Thank you for taking care of all of us during my surgery. Thank you for your friendship. I'm in awe of your capacity to love...and organize! Thanks to Sasha, David, and Emma for holding things down at home while Anya transformed our home and hearts for the better.

To my Aunt Angela and Uncle Sasha, thank you for helping raise me. You brought me joy and comfort and expanded my horizons. Vikey, Andre, Nicole, Oleg, Richie, Jackie—I love you all.

To my family who are not here to hold this book in their hands but who have supported me always: Papa Senya, Baba Raya, Deda Yosya, Baba Frida, Deda Sasha, Baba Laura, Deda Fima, and all those who are sending their highest support, love, and light, thank you for being there.

To My Friends

Life feels more right after we talk. I breathe easier knowing you're by my side. From reading chapters to giving me feedback on the book cover and validating me when I was scared, thank you, Jessica Alpert, Lisa Zigarmi, Marjorie Dickinson, Olga Lemberg, Seth Yalcin, Alina Liberman, and Andrew Sinkov. A+A, extra thanks for housing my writing retreats. I appreciate all the friends who showed up for brainstorms, attended events, made connections, helped me along my long journey, and just kept me and the fam company: Lana and Alex Rovner, Annie Nazarian, Mike Davydov, Leydi and Eddie Roffman, Tanya and George Pushchinsky, Arielle Sigmon, Erez Levin, Cynthia Koons, Karla Lightfoot, Jeffrey Briggs, Christy Liu, Evan Schneyer, Jessica Huang, Claudia Huerta, Kelly Quinley, Jen and Andrew Hall, Hollie Greene, Jim Rottman, Lenny Rachitsky, Michelle Rial, Amy and Adam Odessky, Selena Soo, Sloane Davidson, Alexa Brandt, Jessica Randazza, Erica Berger, Alisa Vitti. Anna Wolf, you started all this by getting me back into coaching. Thank you!

It Takes a Village

There's no fulfillment at work if you can't have proper childcare. I wouldn't be able to do my work if it weren't for great nannies, babysitters, teachers, day cares, and schools. I pray we can transform our systems to make quality childcare and education available to all. A loving thanks to Ida, Samira, Guzel, Cynthia, Elena, Nuria, and Oksana. Thank you, also, to my family for watching the kids when you could.

To My Well-Being Squad

Yolanda Martin, I don't know how I'd make it through without you. I know you say I'd find a way, but I owe much of my growth and transformation to you. Thank you for encouraging me to notice what I notice—that's echoed throughout these pages. Madeline Till, thank you for helping me slow down and sort through my past so I can be more present. Jacqueline Winchester, I'm in awe of your miraculous work; each of our sessions has been a game changer. Janaki Amin, thank you for teaching me how to communicate with my body. Anastasia Bazarova, thank you for your loving support and presence, friendship, and healing. Paula Parker, thank you for screwing my head on straight each time I see you. Melissa Wolfe-Rosebro, thank you for teaching me how to move efficiently. Dr. Shimelfarb, thanks for your deep presence through my difficult times. Karissa, thanks for your intuition and encouragement. Dr. Chi, thanks for your lifesaving work.

To Mappsters, Mentors, and Teachers

Thank you to the Mappster community at large—you all inspire me. I've been quiet and haven't made the annual gatherings in a while, but I feel your kind spirit and am grateful for your work. Thank you to Martin Seligman for founding this field and to Barbara Fredrickson for her research and support throughout the years. Thanks to Beth Schoenfeldt and Victoria Colligan for founding Ladies Who Launch and giving me a chance to participate and help grow such an exciting community of entrepreneurs. Thank you to Belle Frank—for seeing me and encouraging me to spread my wings. Thanks to the

Barnard Writing Fellows program for normalizing the angst of writing. Thank you to my fifth-grade teacher, Mr. B., who quieted the angry boys in my class when I presented my book report on Elizabeth Cady Stanton and argued for a female president. Thank you to my second-grade teacher, Ms. Duffola, for your warmth and nurturing my spelling edge.

To My Clients

For privacy reasons, I won't name you here, but know that you're close in my heart and the source of all of this. Even if it's been decades. To each person I have coached, I'm grateful you trusted me to be a part of your journey. You've taught me so much and informed this work. I love celebrating your celebrations. Keep sending them! To my speaking clients, thank you for the opportunity to support your teams and organizations. Each time I get in front of a group, I leave energized and grateful. You help me live on purpose.

To My Colleagues

Stephanie Wilson, you've kept this business flowing while I've been head down—I couldn't do it without you. Thank you for keeping me organized with my citations. Sean Mandell, thank you for doing the heavy lifting in setting up systems and flows early on in my business. To Kate Zeitler, thanks for your fabulous design. Christine Campione, thanks for generously opening so many doors and, most importantly, becoming a good friend. To Stephan Mardyks, thanks for encouraging me to go for publishing and for helping me get this program out in the world with SM Covey. Thanks to Valorie Burton, Carin Rockind, and Senia Maymin for cheering me on and reading my initial proposal. Senia, thanks for your guidance and introducing me to my agent, Jill Marsal. Thank you to Monica Shah for helping me get my practice off the ground. Thanks to SV Change for being a community that took the lonely edge off writing. Thanks to Ilene Schaffer for reading my boundaries chapter and recommending Theano.

To My Writing Support System

Thanks to Theano Writing Group, including Kathryn Britton, Yashi Srivastava, Kelly Beischel, Aren Cohen, Bess Keller, and Jan Stanley, for giving me loving feedback. Thank you to Sue Shapiro for responding to my emails at all hours of the night—I'm grateful for your perspective and support.

To My Publishing Team

Thank you to my agent, Jill Marsal, for your faith in me, guidance, and kindness. Thank you to my developmental editor, Dan Ambrosio; you made my dream come true. Each call with you left me feeling supported and seen. Thank you to the design, sales, marketing, PR, legal, and editing team at Hachette Go and everyone who touched this book, including Andrew Goldberg, Nzinga Temu, Alison Dalafave, Sean Moreau, Xian Lee, Christina Palaia, Annie Lenth Chatham, Kay Mariea, Kara Brammer, and Lauren Rosenthal. I'm so immensely grateful for your support. I couldn't do this without you. Finally, thank you to Brandi Bowles who first saw that I had a book in me.